John O'Neill

Official Report of Gen. John O'Neill, President of the Fenian Brotherhood

On the attempt to invade Canada, May 25th, 1870. The preparations therefor, and the cause of its failure, with a sketch of his connection with the organization

John O'Neill

Official Report of Gen. John O'Neill, President of the Fenian Brotherhood
On the attempt to invade Canada, May 25th, 1870. The preparations therefor, and the cause of its failure, with a sketch of his connection with the organization

ISBN/EAN: 9783337373412

Printed in Europe, USA, Canada, Australia, Japan

Cover: Foto ©ninafisch / pixelio.de

More available books at **www.hansebooks.com**

OFFICIAL REPORT

OF

GEN. JOHN O'NEILL,

PRESIDENT OF THE FENIAN BROTHERHOOD;

ON THE ATTEMPT TO INVADE CANADA,

MAY 25th, 1870.

The preparations therefor, and the cause of its failure, with a sketch of his connection with the Organization, and the motives which led him to join it:

ALSO

A REPORT OF

THE BATTLE OF RIDGEWAY, CANADA WEST,

FOUGHT JUNE 2nd, 1866, BY COLONEL BOOKER, COMMANDING THE QUEEN'S OWN, AND OTHER CANADIAN TROOPS, AND COLONEL JOHN O'NEILL, COMMANDING THE FENIANS.

NEW YORK:
PUBLISHED BY JOHN J. FOSTER,
512 BROADWAY.
1870.

REPORT OF GENERAL JOHN O'NEILL,

PRESIDENT OF THE FENIAN BROTHERHOOD,

On the attempt to invade Canada, May 25th, 1870, the preparations therefor, and the cause of its failure, with a sketch of his connection with the Organization, and the motives which led him to join it.

IN JAIL AT BURLINGTON, VT., *June 25th, 1870.*

To the officers and members of the Fenian Brotherhood, and the friends of Irish liberty generally:

GENTLEMEN:—Since I last had the honor to address you, an important event in the history of the Organization has occurred: and judging from the general tenor of newspaper reports, the man whom you then most trusted, has, for the time, lost your confidence. While I may be grieved at this, still, conscious of having performed my whole duty as far as in me lay, I have nothing to regret in the past, excepting that those whose co-operation I had looked for, so utterly failed to keep their solemn pledges. Whatever I have done in connection with the Fenian Brotherhood, was done for Ireland, from conviction, and not to please any particular class of persons. If, under similar circumstances, another leader would have done better, I have only to regret that I, and not he, had been selected. You are well aware that far from seeking official position in the Brotherhood, it was thrust upon me in violence to my wishes. Having often received your applause for an act possessing little intrinsic merit, perhaps it is not strange that my acts of real merit should be misunderstood and condemned. Of this, however, you may be assured, I labored arduously and successfully in preparing the Organization for the field, had the arms and war material in the proper place at the proper time, and if the men were not on hand to do the fighting, the fault was not mine. Success or failure is not a fair criterion on which to form one's judgment, and yet you must own that it is thus you have formed your unfavorable opinion of me in relation to the late attempted invasion of Canada.

A firm believer in steel as the cure of Irish grievances, I was attracted to the ranks of the Organization for no other reason than it proposed such a remedy. It was not, however, until the plan of invading Canada was adopted, that I became a member, for I considered the direct invasion of Ireland wholly impracticable, while England remained at peace with her neighbors. Canada once gained, would serve as an excellent base of operations against the enemy; and its acquisition did not seem too great an undertaking, from the number, strength, and resources of our people on the American Continent. There was, too, an army of veteran Irish soldiers but just disbanded by the close of civil conflict in the United States, that were ready and anxious to be led to battle for their country. As to the propriety of invading Canada, I have always had but one opinion: Canada is a province of Great Britain; the English flag floats over it and English soldiers protect it, and, I think, wherever the English flag and English soldiers are found, Irishmen have a right to attack. In striking at England through Canada we attempted no more than was done by the American Republic in the war of the Revolution.

The movement of 1866, for two causes, either one of which had been sufficient, resulted disastrously. The men failed to be on the ground in available numbers at the appointed time, and those who did arrive were unprovided with arms and ammunition; various reasons were assigned for these two grave mishaps, some correct, others incorrect, but nearly all reflecting on the capacity and management of the then commanding general, T. W. Sweeny. The charges then made against General Sweeny have since been repeated, but with more bitterness, against myself. In a movement like ours, if unsuccessful, it seems inevitable that some one has to be made the victim. Disappointed patriots then fail to remember that the leader can only issue orders and instructions, and that prompt compliance therewith becomes their duty. Though the attempt be foiled by their neglect to carry out his orders, they are none the less quick to heap ignominy on his head, forgetful of the fact that they themselves were the chief authors of disaster by their criminal inactivity. In the movement of 1866 I occupied a subordinate position, whose duties I performed to the best of my ability. On the failure of the general plan of campaign I returned, as soon as released by the Federal authorities, to my home in Nashville, Tennessee. Then, and for some time afterwards, I labored quietly in the ranks to prepare another effort, without a thought of official connection with the Brotherhood. On the 1st of January, 1868, Col. W. R. Roberts resigned. At the earnest solicitation of P. J. Meehan and the other leading men of the Organization, and on their representations to me that the very existence of the Fenian Brotherhood depended on my action, I was induced to become its president, not, however, before I had exacted from the Senate of F. B. (fifteen in number,) a solemn promise that they would unite with me in preparing for a fight that year. My labors during the spring and summer of 1868 in addressing private and public meetings throughout the country and in attending at State Conventions from Maine to Minnesota, are well known to you. I was ably seconded in this work by the organizing corps, and also received some assistance from the then vice president of the F. B., James Gibbons—a man whose enthusiastic temperament and lack of judgment often betrayed him into making promises of a speedy fight wholly unwarranted by the state of our preparations. This gentleman has since, however, grown profoundly wise, and under the guidance of P. J. Meehan, the evil genius of Fenianism, was greatly instrumental in bringing about the recent failure—*rule* or *ruin* being the motto of himself and his master. Others of the Senators, instead of giving me the assistance promised, made use of their official position in the Organization to advance themselves politically, and are now occupying lucrative political offices which they could never have otherwise obtained. To such parties it was quite convenient to continue patriotic Fenians for an indefinite period. Before attaining office they were enthusiastic for an early movement against the enemy, but, this point gained, they suddenly changed their tactics and grew hot advocates of slow and cautious measures. Without the honesty or manhood to leave the Organization and openly denounce its schemes as impracticable, they remained apparently faithful to the cause, but at the same time knew how to sow the seeds of dissension and distrust, and to vilify those who had embarked their whole fortunes in the undertaking. This they did, to paralyze the efforts of earnest men and to keep the Brotherhood as a mere machine to help them in working out their own political plans and purposes. The liberation of Ireland through an invasion of Canada had not me for its author; and I very much question if its originators had not lost all faith in it after the failure of the movement of 1866. Be that as it may, it was the plan given me to execute by these men; and believing in its feasibility, I devoted my entire energies to rendering it successful. For this, two things seemed to me absolutely necessary, viz., a sufficient quantity of war material secretly deposited at the several strategic points near the border, and a sufficient number of men to take that war material across the border before the Federal authorities could interfere.

The movement once inaugurated on Canadian soil, I felt that thousands of Irishmen would rush to our aid; and hence, that it was my duty to prepare to strike the first blow successfully, and confide in the patriotism of my countrymen to do the rest. Two years and a half of my life were devoted to this preparation. Having but one object in view in becoming a Fenian or accepting official position in the Organization, and, as far as my personal interests were concerned, with everything to lose and nothing to gain, I was determined to test the practicability of the movement, for at best it was but an experiment. I was painfully aware that the longer we waited, the less confidence would the Organization and the Irish people generally have in our ability to succeed: and besides, the thousands of our countrymen who participated in the late war, were fast settling down in life, and if we deferred matters much longer, it would be almost impossible to secure a sufficient number of veteran soldiers for the proper inauguration of the movement.

The Senate, or rather the master spirit of that body, P. J. Meehan, finding that I was really in earnest, went to work in his own peculiar style to foil my efforts by seeking to destroy my influence with the Organization and ruining my character. No Irishman in America is better qualified for such *honorable* work; and no one had better facilities, having his own organ, the *Irish American*, with the *United Irishman* and the *Irish Republic* to support his malignant assaults. In this attack upon me, he found willing tools in many of his confreres in the Senate. They threw every obstacle in the way of the movement that might retard it, while they sought to fix on me all the responsibility of delay, and thus hurt my character and bring the Organization to look on them as the only parties worthy its confidence.

I will here state that my first call for a Congress to meet in New York, April 19th, 1870, and some of the subsequent circulars were intended to deceive the

American and Canadian governments as to our real intentions. I intended to make a move before the convening of the above Congress, but could not make that fact known to all the members of the Senate, as I had reason to fear that some of them would betray the secret. Richard McCloud, one of these political Senators, happened to learn my purpose, and, as it served his interest to delay matters, forthwith communicated the affair to the newspapers—hence the scare across the border in April last. At every step in my preparations I had to encounter the most stubborn and persistent opposition from Mr. Meehan and his friends, who, while clamoring for a forward movement and passing resolutions to that effect—(see resolutions sent to circles by the Senate during the past two years)—were privately doing all in their power to frustrate the efforts made by me in the direction of a fight. During the past winter months competent and reliable men, Colonels Henry Le Caron and William Clingen were employed in locating our arms, etc., at convenient points along the border, and when everything was on the eve of completion, I called a Congress of the Brotherhood to meet in New York, March 8th, 1870. In this call I had to indicate too clearly the object of the previous call. The time for assembling the General Congress, in accordance with the Constitution, had been suffered to pass, as it was the opinion of P. J. Meehan, James Gibbons, myself, and such others of the Senators as I could advise with, that, instead of convening the regular Congress, we should go on with our preparations. Besides, the removal of the munitions of war which was then proceeding, required a degree of secrecy that would have been endangered by the open discussion of delegates; and no subsequent Congress could be brought together in strict accordance with the Constitution of the F. B. It was my intention to lay a full and complete statement of the condition and resources of the Organization before the delegates, and appeal to them to furnish the means necessary to perfect our arrangements —breech-loading ammunition being the principal article needed. Mr. Meehan & Co. were, however, determined, if possible, to prevent the assembling of the delegates, as they quite well knew that the Congress would furnish all that the Senate had previously declared to be necessary for the inauguration of the movement. Letters received from every side fully indicated that the approaching Fenian Congress would be far the largest ever gathered together, and would by its decided action remove every pretext for further delay in taking the field. At a meeting of the Senate held in February last, it was therefore resolved to forbid the assembling of the delegates, and orders to that effect were issued on the 28th of that month, with the information added, that they would soon call a Congress of their own. They had previously carried off the books of the Brotherhood to the apartment of Richard McCloud, where their session was held on Sunday, the 27th of February, under pretence of vacating their rooms at headquarters for the use of the military officers of the district; but in reality to get possession of said books and papers preparatory to breaking up the Organization and establishing one of their own. Their scheme was to have a Congress got together in some far-off Western city, whither the circles in the Eastern States would be unwilling, on account of expense, to send delegates, and where they might have a sufficient number of adherents to carry out their projects, or, failing in that, effectually destroy and disrupt the Organization. It is quite evident that all the Senators were not aware of the designs of Mr. Meehan, and it is no easy matter to measure the man accurately, as no one can play the hypocrite with more taking simplicity. The insane attempt on the life of Mr. Meehan occurring the same evening on which he and his satellites determined to forbid the attendance of the delegates at the approaching Congress, and to call one of their own instead—an attempt regretted by none more than myself, in spite of the lying insinuations of Meehan and his friends—placed me in an extremely embarrassing position. It was then a generally well known fact that, since the Philadelphia Congress of November, 1868, the greater portion of the funds of the Organization had passed through the hands of Mr. Meehan, as he had entire control of the factory and of the payments made for the alterations of arms. The amount of money so expended was a cause of great dissatisfaction in the Organization, as it reached a sum nearly double that reported by Mr. Meehan, as necessary at the Philadelphia Congress. Under such circumstances, I felt it would not be just to the latter to have a Congress meet and pass upon his accounts, while he was, for aught we knew to the contrary, on his death-bed. Up to that hour, I had received no written report from Mr. Meehan, and his verbal reports had been loose and unsatisfactory. Subsequently, the clerk of the Senate sent me a copy of what purported to be a partial report, which had probably been approved by that body. I will venture the assertion, however, that there is not a business man in the country who would accept it, as in any sense a satisfactory report for the expenditure of so much money. It is a little strange that a man who has set himself up as a model patriot, the guardian of the hard earned money of our people, and the strict accountant of every cent of Fenian money that passed through the hands of others, should be so lax in dealing with himself. Mr. Meehan's accounts and vouchers for the expenditure of over sixty thousand dollars of this same hard-earned money, have not, as yet, to my knowledge, been subjected to an examination. Will the white-washing committee that reported on this matter at the Convention held in Chicago last April, have the hardihood to assert that they examined a single one of Mr. Meehan's vouchers? and, if they did not, will they be kind enough to inform the Fenian Brotherhood what documents, or evidence of any kind, were submitted to them that will go to justify them in the report they made? But I forget; Messrs. Hynes and McCloud were there; it would be queer if evidence should be wanting, with their inventive fancy to call on. It is curious, however, that none of the numerous Financial Committees of the Senate examined his accounts. Mr. Meehan stated that he had the vouchers, or, at least, the greater portion of them, in his possession when the Congress met in New York, but, being handed into that body shortly before its adjournment, they were referred to the Executive Committee of the F. B., and, as they never afterwards met, no action was ever taken with regard to those vouchers. I would now respectfully suggest that the Finance Committee of the next Congress investigate this matter, and that Mr. E. A. Cole, the foreman of the factory, and J. P. B * * * * *, the assistant secretary of the treasury and book-keeper during most of the time that Mr. Meehan was drawing money, be called upon to assist them in their labors. I have no doubt but that Mr. Meehan can submit a very plausible report, since he is quite as expert in white-washing as in defamation; still, it will do no harm to have his vouchers examined, that it may be known to whom and for what purposes so much money was paid out. As one who labored unweariedly night and day in collecting most of this money, I may be pardoned the desire to find out how it was expended.

But to return. The Senate had now in its possession the important books and papers of the organization, and were, as I knew, determined to retain them. The unfortunate attempt on the life of Mr. Meehan would serve them as a pretext to refuse attendance on the Congress called by me. Under all the circumstances of the case I deemed it most expedient to unite with the Senate in the call for a Congress to be held at Chicago, Ills., April 11th, 1870, being under the impression that the Senate, in compliance with the professed desire of Mr. Meehan, would act in accord with me in carrying out the oft-declared mission of the Brotherhood. No sooner, however, had I joined in the call, (which was written by one of themselves, P. W. Dunne, and contained a fulsome eulogium on Mr. Meehan,) than the friends of the latter commenced a bitter and vindictive assault upon my character, which he and they have continued to this day. This display of petty malice proved to me at once that far from aiding, they would throw every obstacle in the way of a fight. I then decided, after receiving assurances of assistance from parties, who subsequently, however, grew less zealous, to carry out the original plan of invading Canada before the 19th of April, and, in the meantime, to deceive enemies and traitors alike, kept up a show of preparing for the Congress already called. Unfortunately, few of our people will bestir themselves until they are fully let into the secret; and, on the present occasion, to procure the needed help, I had to make known my plans to so many that the enemy got wind of what I was about. I was thus compelled to abandon for a time a forward movement, and was forced into the Congress held at New York, April 19th, 1870. As I expected to be in quite a different quarter when this Congress should convene, I had made no preparations for it, and had, in fact, prevented many circles from sending on delegates. Though the attendance was thus not so large as it might have been, the Organization was quite fairly represented. Nearly all the letters then received, indicated that the Organization demanded and would sustain an immediate movement. The Senate party had previously met in Chicago. That honorable body, or, at least, the portion of it present, to wit, James Gibbons, Wm. J. Hynes, Richard McCloud, and P. W. Dunne, true to their natural instincts, and ambitious to excel their master, exhausted the calendar of crimes in their effort to bring disgrace on the President of the Fenian Brotherhood, and cloak their own treason. It is hardly necessary for me to say that the charges preferred, and the evidence adduced to establish them, are pure fabrications. In spite of the great ado made in the newspapers, very few of the circles attached to the organization sent delegates to Chicago. Now, however, the men there elected to official position, very modestly claim to be the sole and only representatives of the Brotherhood. They profess to have broken up the old Organization and built a new one out of the ruins. After forming a Governing Council of nine, they appointed a special committee of three to attend the Congress called by me in New York, and insisted that the Constitution adopted by them in Chicago, should be accepted by us without the least modification or change. This insulting proposition was, of course, rejected. My re-election to the Presidency of the F. B., then followed, which I accepted on the express understanding that I should go on perfectly free and untramelled in the work of preparing the Organization for a fight. The Financial Committee of the Congress recommended that thirty thousand dollars be collected within seven days to meet contingent expenses, and complete our preparations. About two thousand dollars of this sum was paid into the treasury before I left New York. I did not deem it necessary to wait the collection of the full amount, as I was satisfied, as soon as we advanced across the border and took up a position there, all the money needed for breech-loading ammunition, the principal deficiency, would be forthcoming. All the necessary arrangements had been made for the delivery of ammunition according as it was purchased. About this time Gen. John H. Gleeson, of Virginia, came to see me, as he said, to make inquiries about the Organization, and to ascertain if we meant to fight; and on learning that such was our purpose, and that the only thing particularly deficient was breech-loading ammunition, offered on the spot to advance ten thousand dollars, and soon after, at a meeting of the officers of the District of Manhattan, renewed the offer, and added five thousand more, but after a few days during which he claimed to be negotiating his farm in Virginia for New York property, he, to the surprise of some few, changed his mind as to the donation. I must now regard his offer as a piece of braggadocio quite in keeping with his subsequent conduct along the border, where he and his "staff" and "detectives," figured quite prominently during the excitement.

Some time before the movement was actually inaugurated, the efforts of the Senate to demoralize the Organization in sowing the seeds of dissension, had begun to have effect. Some of the men who had previously expressed the greatest impatience for a fight, now that it was at hand, were most active in their opposition. These worthies, though they had boasted often and loud of their desire to die battling for Ireland, as the hour approached to realize their boast, showed a manifest inclination to snuff the battle afar off, and anxiously looked for an excuse to cover up their cowardice. The action of the Senate furnished them with that excuse. We hope they are satisfied with themselves; they can now, at least, talk away to their hearts' content of their valorous impulses without any fear of having them soon brought to a test in a fight for Ireland.

The military men who were ordered to put themselves in readiness to move previous to the sitting of the Congress, were now becoming very impatient, especially those in New York, Brooklyn, and Boston. This was not to be wondered at, as many of them had given up their occupations, while the civil members of the two former cities had fallen away greatly from the zeal and activity displayed by them during the Congress. Much of the discontent and apathy which prevailed in New York and Brooklyn, is to be attributed to the constitutional fault-finding of a miserable fellow just elected to the post of Vice President of the Fenian Brotherhood. His sole ambition seemed to be, to have matters so arranged as to have himself recognized the head and front of Fenianism in my absence. Unhappily, it has occurred but too frequently in the Organization, that members were willing to sacrifice the cause to advance their own interests. To satisfy his petty ambition and stop his slanderous talk, I remained in New York for two weeks previous to the movement, when my presence elsewhere was absolutely needed, to get the men in readiness and complete our arrangements. As a consequence, many points which Gen. Donnelly and myself intended visiting personally, and on which we depended for men to inaugurate the movement, could not be reached; hence the failure of those men to arrive in time, and, in a great measure, the failure of the movement. Matters were in such a condition when I finally had it in my power to leave New York, that an advance became at once imperative. Thus I was compelled to relinquish my intention of visiting the West publicly and then quietly return after having seen all the officers in whom I confided for effective aid at the outset. The author of this mischievous delay was elected Vice President solely because he was thought friendly to myself, and his harmonious co-operation would free me from the obstacles previously thrown in the way of perfecting my arrangements. His duplicity during the sitting of the Congress favored this opinion. Had the Congress the least reason to think otherwise, his election would never have occurred. I had already, however, learned to appreciate the man and would never have consented to act as President, with him as my next superior officer, had I not anticipated taking the field at an early day. Once the advance in the field, the mission of the Fenian Brotherhood was ended. All the branches of the F. B. combined, could not keep twenty thousand men in the field thirty days. Whoever opines to the contrary, merely shows his profound ignorance of the resources required to support an army in active service. The supremely wise statesmen of the Senate, with a few others, imagined, no doubt, that they were the only persons fitted to express an opinion on this subject. As for myself, I looked to Irishmen and friends of Irish liberty all over the world, for the aid that would enable us to cope with any degree of success against the great power of England. Men of means and influence there are in great abundance, who have never touched Fenianism, yet sympathize deeply with Irish freedom; these, once effective action was begun, would be the foremost among the active allies of belligerent Ireland. The efforts that have been made to contract Fenianism, and keep it within the complete control of a few pretended patriots, have proved its greatest weakness.

The following resolutions of the Senate of the Fenian Brotherhood, on the subject of a fight, adopted at the various meetings of that body, are copied from the proceedings of the Senate.

The names of the Senators elected at the Cleveland Congress, September, 1868, are as follows:

Thomas Lavan, Cleveland, Ohio; James Gibbons, Philadelphia, Pa.; T. J. Quinn, Albany, N. Y.; Miles D. Sweeney, San Francisco, Cal.; John Carlton, Bordentown, N. J.; Frank B. Gallagher, Buffalo, N. Y.; P. W. Dunne, Peoria, Illinois; Edward L. Carey, New York City; Patrick J. Meehan, Hoboken, N. J.; Peter Cunningham, Utica, N. Y.; Michael Finnegan, Haughton, Michigan; J. C. O'Brien, Rochester, N. Y.; William Fleming, Troy, N. Y.; James W. Fitzgerald, Cincinnati, Ohio; John O'Niell, Washington, D. C. John O'Niell succeeded Col. W. R. Roberts, as President, January 1st, 1868. Thomas Lavan resigned July, 1868. Patrick Bannon, of Louisville, Ky., and Patrick Sweeney, of Lawrence, Mass., were appointed in July, 1868, to the positions vacated by O'Niell and Lavan.

SENATE RESOLUTIONS.

"*New York*, January 1, 1868.

* * * * * * * *

"Mr. P. J. Meehan offered the following resolution :

"*Resolved*, That this Senate hereby pledge themselves to the members of the Fenian Brotherhood, and to each other, to go to work at once to put the national organization on a war footing; that they will spare no personal effort or exertion that can be made to that end; and that as soon as the military organization can be put on an effective footing, the fight for the freedom of Ireland shall be commenced without delay. Motion seconded by E. L. Carey and carried.

"It was moved and carried that the absent members of the Senate, and all Organizers and Circles be informed of the above resolution, and invited to co-operate therein."

* * * * * * * *

Senators present—James Gibbons, P. J. Meehan, Frank B. Gallagher, John Carlton, Michael Cunningham, William Fleming, J. C. O'Brien, Edward L. Carey, all of whom voted for the resolutio

"*New York*, January 4, 1868.

* * * * * * * *

"*Resolved*, That should John Savage, Esq., refuse to fulfill the agreement with the President and Senate of the F. B., entered into on the 13th of December, 1867, it is the sense of this Senate, that a vigorous prosecution of the war policy adopted by them on the 1st of January, 1868, affords the best guarantee of a real union of Irish nationalists, and to that end they pledge themselves anew to carry out that policy, and to sustain the President of the F. B. in his efforts to give it practical effect."

The ayes and nays were called for, and the following vote taken: Ayes, Senators Gallagher, Cunningham, Carey, Carlton, Quinn, O'Brien, Meehan, and Gibbons. Nays, none.

* * * * * * * *

"*New York*, January 5, 1868.

* * * * * * * *

"Mr. J. C. O'Brien offered the following resolution :

"*Resolved*, That the members of the Senate, with the President of the F. B., on and after the 25th of January, 1868, go out and publicly and privately appeal to our people for the aid necessary to put an army in the field. That where practicable, a senator be accompanied by an organizer, and that they make an especial effort to procure from citizens of the various localities, means to transport to the front, the men raised in each locality."

"The resolution was seconded and unanimously adopted."

* * * * * * * *

Senators present—Gibbons, Gallagher, Cunningham, Meehan, Carey, Carlton, Quinn, and O'Brien. Jas. W. Fitzgerald, P. W. Dunne, and Thomas Lavan, who were not present when the foregoing resolutions passed the Senate, subsequently pledged themselves to sustain them, and assist in carrying them out.

Buffalo, N. Y., July 23, 1868.

* * * * * * * *

"The following preamble and resolutions were presented and seconded:

"*Whereas*, the Senate of the Fenian Brotherhood at the session of their body on the first of January, 1868, adopted a resolution expressing their determination to put the Military Organization on an effective war footing as speedily as possible, and, that as soon as this should be accomplished, the fight for the independence of Ireland should commence; and, *Whereas*, with a view to accomplish this end, conventions of the Brotherhood have been called in all the States in which such assemblies were possible, at which the delegates of the circles there represented, pledged themselves in the name of their several circles, to raise, and forward to head-quarters before the 15th of July, the means necessary to place an army in the field, but from the financial report now before the Senate, it appears that only one fourth of the amount so promised had been received up to the 10th of July, and as money is absolutely necessary to complete the preparations on which success depends: therefore,

"*Resolved*, That the Senate being decidedly in favor of the immediate commencement of the fight for the liberation of Ireland, pledge themselves individually to go out amongst the members of the Organization, and those who sympathize with the cause of Ireland, and use all their influence and every possible effort to raise the balance of the money required to make a forward movement, and that they further pledge themselves to the Organization, that as soon as the necessary means are placed in their hands, an army shall be marched into the enemy's country under the green flag of Ireland, and military preparations shall not be delayed a single day.

"*Resolved*, That the Executive Committee of the Senate, in connection with the President of the Fenian Brotherhood, be empowered and directed to correspond and negotiate with as many of the military men who were engaged on either side of the late war, together with such other parties as they may think proper, to the end that their military services or pecuniary aid may be procured, to render an immediate forward movement practicable, and if, in the judgment of said committee and president, the military services and pecuniary aid required, are forthcoming to their satisfaction, then they are hereby empowered and directed to make such necessary arrangements on behalf of the Senate as to direct and aid the president in taking the preliminary steps for said movement, and further, that, if said time be considered propitious, then the president is hereby requested to call a meeting of the Senate as soon as practicable, after any definite time of action may be settled upon by said committee, and that said committee be empowered to select any member of the Senate to aid in carrying into effect the spirit of this resolution.

"*Resolved*, That in the event of the efforts being made to raise the means wherewith to commence a forward movement should prove unsuccessful within the next four months, then it is hereby declared that, from the encouraging reports made by the president and Executive Committee on the subject of certain negotiations with prominent military men of this country, and their promise to render valuable personal assistance within a given time, this, together with the legitimate resources to be derived from the various circles of the Fenian Brotherhood, justify the Senate in their settled determination, to attack the enemy with an organized force, at as early a day next spring as the weather will permit, and to this end, said Executive Committee, in connection with the president of the F. B. be, and they are hereby empowered to take any and all necessary steps towards placing the Organization in a position to take the field at the time above indicated."

The resolutions were unanimously adopted.

* * * * * * * *

Senators present—Gibbons, Carlton, Finnegan, Gallagher, Flemming, Carey, Meehan, Cunningham, O'Brien, and Fitzgerald.

At the General Congress held in Philadelphia, November, 1868, nine Senators were elected, who, with the six holding over, made the Senate consist of the following gentlemen:

F. B. Gallagher, Buffalo, N. Y.; E. L. Carey, New York; T. J. Quinn, Albany, N. Y.; James Gibbons, Philadelphia, Pa.; P. W. Dunne, Peoria, Ill.; M. D. Sweeney, San Francisco, Cal.; J. W. Fitzgerald, Cincinnati, Ohio; T. McKinley, Nashville, Tenn.; R. McCloud, Norwich, Ct.; J. E. Downey, Providence, R. I.; P. Bannon, Louisville, Ky.; William J. Hynes, Washington, D. C.; P. J. Meehan, Hoboken, N. J.; John O'Neill, Dubuque, Iowa; J. C. O'Brien, Rochester, N. Y.

John O'Neill resigned August, 1869, and Wm. J. Davis, of Brooklyn, N. Y., was appointed to fill his place.

RESOLUTIONS PASSED SUBSEQUENT TO THE PHILADELPHIA CONGRESS.

Pittsburgh, Pa., July 1st, 1869.

* * * * * * * *

"On motion, the following resolutions were adopted:

"*Resolved*, That in accordance with the plan of action, and policy determined on by the Senate in secret session, the President and Ex. Com. are hereby instructed to take immediate steps to insure the harmonious and united action of the Irish people, both in America and Ireland, and wherever our people are to be found throughout the Dominion of England, and that all details in reference to these matters be referred to the President, and Ex. Com. till the next meeting of the Senate.

Resolved, That an address be issued by the Senate to the members of the F. B., urging on them to go to work at once, and help to carry out the policy determined on, and which, if vigorously sustained and prosecuted, cannot fail to give freedom and national standing to the Irish race."

I was informed that the "plan of action and policy determined on in secret session" was to inaugurate the movement that fall, and each of the Senators present again pledged himself to go out in his respective locality, and raise the necessary means to complete our preparations, and to meet in New York on the 10th of the following month, to make final arrangements, and remain in session until the army took the field. Senators present—Gibbons, Gallagher, Quinn, Carey, McCloud, Meehan, Dunne, and McKinley.

New York, Aug., 19, 1869.

* * * * * * * *

"On motion of J. W. Fitzgerald, as much of the proceedings in Ex. session as are embraced in the following resolutions, were ordered to be placed on record :

"*Resolved*, as the sense of the Senate F. B., that we commence military operations at the earliest day practicable, upon the receipt of twenty-five thousand dollars, upon the basis of resolution adopted in Executive session, at the meeting of the Senate at Pittsburg, Pa., and that the members of the Senate apply themselves at once to the raising of said amount in their respective districts."

Senators present—Gibbons, Meehan, Fitzgerald, McCloud, Downey, Carey, Hynes, O'Brien, Quinn, and Davis.

IMMEDIATE PREPARATIONS BEFORE TAKING THE FIELD.

AWARE of how important it was for our ultimate success, that, by a secret and simultaneous movement, our men should be thrown across the border in numbers sufficient to take and hold certain strategic points, before either government was apprised of our design, or at least, before they could interfere with effect, I had the preparations for taking the field conducted with the greatest silence and secrecy, using every possible precaution to throw them off their guard. About three weeks previous to the movement, I issued a general order, a copy of which was sent to each circle and to the proper military officers, instructing them to hold their men in readiness to move at a moment's notice, and ten days before going to the border, I sent a letter to the military officers, ordering them to provide at once the means of transportation for their men, as final orders would be forwarded them in a few days. Several days after, a communication was directed to the military officers and such of the circles as had reported within the year to head-quarters, to send on their men Monday night, May 23rd, to Malone or St. Albans, as either point happened to be more convenient. This latter communication was mailed in time to have it reach the circles from twelve to forty-eight hours before the time appointed for starting. The circles in the large cities, where the facilities for receiving communications and concentrating men were best, and where, also the chances of having our plans discovered were greatest, received the shortest notice. I desired to give a longer notice, but the danger of having our efforts nipped in the bud through the indiscreet remarks of officers and men, were too great ; besides, the notices previously sent were, in my judgment, amply sufficient. All were ordered to leave home the same night—those near the border as well as those at a distance—for the evident reason that the railroads near the line (with which I did not dare to make arrangements for fear of discovery) would not otherwise be able to accommodate our men if they came in the numbers expected. Besides, the moment those of our men who lived at distant points left for the front, our intention would no longer be a secret to either government, as the fact would be telegraphed at once all over the country. The time of departure for our men in the extreme Western States and territories, who were to operate against the Red River Expedition, was left with the officers in charge.

Apart from the provisions made, as stated, to secure a sufficient body of troops to begin the campaign, I relied chiefly on the men from Massachusetts, Rhode Island, Vermont, and Northeastern New York. Gen. J. J. Donnelly, speaking in behalf of the Organization in the two former States, assured me that he would have from ten to twelve hundred men at, or near St. Albans, on the morning of Tuesday, May 24th; Col. E. C. Lewis, on behalf of the latter, gave me a like assurance of six hundred men at the place and time indicated. These were to be followed up by an equal force within twenty-four hours. These officers had been specially assigned to organize in their respective localities, and viewed in this light, the truth of their assertions was not to be doubted; with these forces increased by considerable bodies which were expected from other quarters, I would have under my command in this section on Wednesday morning upwards of four thousand men. If all, or even half of these had arrived in time, the result would have been quite different. From a thousand to fifteen hundred men were in the meantime to assemble at Malone.

I arrived in the vicinity of St. Albans Sunday morning, May 22d, while nearly every newspaper in the country had me on my way to Chicago, to consult with Riel's agent from the Red River settlement. Their information in this particular was about as correct as that from which were made up their reports of the affair at Eccles Hill, and the manner of my arrest. From personal inspection, I found that the arrangements for getting the arms and ammunition up in proper time were complete. Similar arrangments had been made at Malone.

PLAN OF CAMPAIGN.

To capture St. Johns, on the Richelieu River, twenty-one miles from the line and twenty-two miles from Montreal, and Richmond in Richmond Co., where that branch of the Grand Trunk R. R., from Portland, Me., connects with the main road, seventy-six miles from Montreal and ninety-six miles from Quebec.

It was my intention to have sent Gen. J. J. Donnelly, with some five hundred men, armed with breech-loaders, and a good supply of ammunition, which was all ready, through on the train Tuesday morning from St. Albans to Rouse's Point, and there seize the train from St. Johns, having previously made arrangements to have one or two rails taken up, so as to prevent its escape, and, if possible, to run into, and capture St. Johns, which at that time was entirely undefended, and contained a considerable amount of arms, etc. If, by any accident, the train could not be seized or used for the purpose intended, then they were to proceed on foot as rapidly as possible, and if they could not capture, they could, at least, threaten the town, and, falling back a short distance, await reinforcements. At the same time a detachment of two hundred men from Rhode Island and other points, were to proceed by way of Island Pond to Richmond, and capture it.

I intended taking the balance of the men (from ten to thirteen hundred) to Franklin, Vt., some 14 miles from St. Albans, and cross the line at Eccles Hill, and proceed toward St. Johns, on the east side of Richelieu River as rapidly as possible, while the men who were ordered to assemble at or near Malone, N. Y., were to proceed to St. Johns by the most direct route on the west side of the river, throwing out a small force of cavalry in the direction of Montreal so as to threaten it. The men coming up all the time, would be in a position to protect the rear. We had hoped to be able to mount a few hundred men immediately on crossing the line. With St. Johns and Richmond in our possession, a partial destruction of railroad communication would have rendered it very difficult for the enemy to concentrate a force sufficient to drive us back, before the thousands who, we believed, would come to our assistance, could reach us. In a further advance, we would, of course have to be guided by the number of the reinforcements that might arrive, and by the number and disposition of the enemy. If we did not succeed in taking and holding Richmond, we could, with a few cavalry, destroy the railroad sufficiently to prevent any force coming from Quebec, at least for a short time, and if we did not succeed in taking either Richmond or St. Johns, we intended to get as far into the country at first, as possible, delay the advance of the enemy, and fall back on our own forces coming up, and when we felt justified in offering or accepting battle, to do so. A small force was ordered to cross at Detroit, Mich., mount themselves, and make a raid through the country, for the purpose of calling attention from other points. At the same time a force was ordered from the extreme Western States and territories, to harass and annoy the Red River expedition on its march, and, if President Riel would fight, to assist him in resisting it, both on the march and on its arrival in the Winnepeg country. It was my intention to order crossings in small detachments at various other points, simply for the purpose of distracting the enemy, and preventing him from concentrating his forces at the main points.

THE FAILURE OF THE MEN TO COME UP.

The failure of the men to come up in anything like the numbers promised and expected, disarranged all my plans. I was in St. Albans Tuesday morning, May 24th, when the 6 o'clock train from the south arrived, bringing, instead of from ten to twelve hundred men promised by Massachusetts, about twenty-five or thirty, including Col. H. Sullivan. He and most of the men he had with him would have served the cause by remaining at home. In lieu of six hundred men promised by Vermont and N. E. New York, about eighty or ninety in charge of Major J. J. Monaghan, arrived on the train. A company of sixty-five men from Burlington, Vt., under command of Capts. William Cronin and Thos. Murphy, had arrived the previous evening, and were sent to Franklin, about 14 miles northeast of St. Albans, and two miles from the Canadian line. I had of course to abandon the idea of taking St. Johns by surprise, which could have been easily done, as up to the last moment the enemy had no knowledge of our movements, so secretly had everything been managed. However, as I expected the arrival of reinforcements that evening from all the New England States, and a portion of the States of New York and New Jersey, (including New York city and Brooklyn,) to the number of fifteen hundred or two thousand men, (the newspaper and telegraphic reports of the number of men on the road, confirming this expectation,) I decided to concentrate all the force I could collect, at or near Franklin, cross the line and take up a position at once. I sent an officer to Malone with instructions to the ranking officer there, to move out, when he got his men ready, in the direction of St. Johns. By appearing to move on St. Johns from these two points, Malone and Franklin, I hoped to divide the enemy's forces, believing that he would move with the larger force to meet the column from Malone, so as to more effectually cover St. Johns and Montreal. I left General Donnelly at St. Albans with instructions to stop all our men going through on their way to Malone, and send them with those who had been ordered to St. Albans, direct to Franklin, and proceeded there myself by way of Fairfield Centre, where I arrived at 3 o'clock in the afternoon. I took this circuitous route to Franklin in order to keep the enemy in ignorance of my whereabouts. Here I found a few of the Burlington men in charge of a small portion of arms, etc., and about half way between this town and the border, on the roadside, at a place called Hubbard's Corner, the balance of the men with the greater portion of the arms, etc. These arms, etc., had been hauled to the above points by citizens of the neighborhood, friendly to the cause, all of whom will please accept my thanks on behalf of the Brotherhood, for their unpaid and untiring exertions on this and on other occasions. I would like to mention names, but fear that it might not be to their interest to do so.

At this time the enemy had no force near the line to oppose us, and I made all necessary arrangements to cross over during the night or early the next morning, taking up a position on Eccles Hill, which I knew to be an admirable one for defence, and one from which the enemy could not dislodge us without artillery, unless, indeed, he had a much superior force. I also intended occupying Cook's Corner, two miles beyond. I was very anxious to get the arms, etc., and a sufficient number of men to protect them on the other side beyond the reach of the United States authorities, whom I desired to evade.

I knew that if we had a good position on the other side of the line, our own men would find their way to us by some means or other. I had intended sending Gen. Donnelly to Malone on Wednesday, to command the troops advancing from that point, with instructions to go as far into the country in the direction of St. Johns as he deemed safe, leaving the principal portion of the arms, etc., behind him, close to the line, and, if pressed by the enemy, to fall back fighting, so as to delay him as long as possible, whilst I should attack with the superior numbers which I supposed would come up to my aid, whatever force might be sent against myself. I felt fully satisfied that the occupation of Canadian territory with any considerable force, would have brought to our assistance all the men and material needed. It is idle now to talk of what we could have done on the other side if we had got a respectable force across, but I am inclined to the opinion that, had such been the case, the Canadian volunteers would not have quite so much to boast of to-day. I might here mention that there were many military officers outside of the Organization and a few in it, of acknowledged ability, who were waiting orders, and who would have been with us in a few days had we been at all successful—amongst the latter, the best and ablest was Gen. M. Kerwin. Apart from those, however, there were some of the first military men of America, who had from time to time promised to assist us once we commenced the work. But we had talked so much, and boasted so loudly, in the past, and had really accomplished so little that they would have nothing to do with us until we gave them some practical evidence of our sincerity. Some men, calling themselves officers, came of their own accord; they would have served the cause by remaining at home and attending to their own business, if they had any. Many of those boasting military titles would have found themselves in the ranks had we got on the other side. Late in the afternoon, the greater portion of the men who left St. Albans in the morning, arrived in camp at Hubbard's Corner. I sent Col. Henry Le Caron, Adjt.-Gen. of the F. B., to St. Albans, to hurry on the men who arrived on the 6 o'clock evening train, so that I might be able to cross the line with a respectable force, either that night or early the next morning. I stopped in Franklin for the night. At 2 o'clock the next morning, Gen. Donnelly—who had been cautioned against remaining in St. Albans any longer, as the U. S. Marshal began to suspect who he was, and might order his arrest—reached town, and reported that between four and five hundred of our men had arrived at St. Albans on the train of the previous evening, and were then but a few hours' march from Franklin. Previous to his arrival, I had received many conflicting reports, all of them exaggerated, of the number of men who were on the way from St. Albans to join us. Gen. Donnelly's report I considered reliable; he, however, was mistaken, as not over two hundred and thirty or forty men arrived on the train; about sixty or seventy of that number under Maj. Danl. Murphy, of Connecticut, arrived at 5 o'clock in the morning, having lost the right road during the night. They travelled some seven miles out of their way. A few men under Capt. Kenally of Marlboro, Mass., also arrived. The balance of the men under Col. John Leddy, of New York, taking another road, had to march nineteen miles, and did not get to camp until one o'clock, except two men who arrived before I started to cross the line. This delay, under the circumstances, is inexcusable.

General Donnelly also reported to me, that the telegraphic dispatches received at St. Albans before he left, announced that one thousand men were on the road from the South, and were expected in St. Albans on the 6 o'clock train in the morning. He left an order with a reliable man at St. Albans, instructing them to get off at St. Albans and march to Franklin at once. The fact was that there were only about sixty of our men on the train, and they kept on to Malone. On hearing that there were so many of our men so near at hand, I determined to defer the crossing until later in the morning, so as to allow at least a portion of those said to be on the road, time to arrive. I permitted Gen. Donnelly to remain with me that morning and take part in the contemplated crossing, after which I intended sending him on to Malone.

PREPARATIONS FOR CROSSING.

About 10.30 o'clock on Wednesday morning, Gen. Geo. P. Foster, United States Marshal, with his deputy, Thos. Failey, accompanied by a number of citizens, came to camp. I at once had my men formed into line with the intention of resisting arrest in case the marshal attempted it, and, in fact, intended arresting himself and his deputy and taking them along if they undertook to interfere with us. The marshal, in his carriage, was stopped by the guard just as he came up to our men. I sent Gen. Donnelly to him, to inform him that it would be useless for him to attempt to make any arrests, as we were prepared to resist it. Gen. Donnelly, however, surmised that the marshal realized the situation, and did not care to interfere with us just then.

I was subsequently informed that he telegraphed to Washington, informing the authorities there, that he was powerless to make any arrests. After some conversation, the marshal expressed a desire to read the President's proclamation, to which Gen. Donnelly objected, and at the same time informed him that we had already seen it; he then requested that the road, being a public highway, be kept clear, so that citizens could pass and repass, which request was at once complied with. I might here mention that a number of citizens were hanging around us, and several buggies, carriages, etc., were continually passing and repassing to the Canadian side, and of course carrying information to the enemy; no doubt several officers came across; this we could not very well avoid without arresting them, which we did not wish to do on American soil.

The marshal came into camp, and Gen. Donnelly informed me that he, the marshal, had no intention of making any arrests, as he had no force with him, and suggested that I had better see him. This I had no objection to, as I was standing in front of some of my men who were drawn up in line under arms. At first, I apprehended that the marshal might have arranged with the citizens to assist him in making arrests, and I desired, if possible, to avoid any difficulty on this side the line. I would not, under any circumstances, permit myself to be arrested while I had means to resist it. The principal conversation I had with the marshal, which occupied perhaps three minutes, was on the subject of keeping the road clear for the passage of citizens. I also told him that I would soon be out of his way. I had nearly two hundred men in or near camp at this time. The marshal then drove across the line to the point where the enemy's forces were in position. When we were advancing we met him returning, and I supposed he kept on to Franklin.

The presence of the United States marshal in camp, with the report that United States soldiers were on their way and close at hand to assist him, together with the fact that I knew the enemy would use every effort to bring up reinforcements to defend the admirable position which by this time he had taken on Eccles Hill, just across the line, caused me to determine on feeling his position at once, and ascertaining more correctly his strength, and, if possible, drive him from the hill. At this time there were many conflicting reports as to his numbers, varying from thirty to three hundred men. Most of the reports, however, agreed in placing his numbers at less than one hundred. We moved out about 11.30 o'clock, A.M., 176 men. A few were left with the war material in camp and in Franklin, and also a few men from Connecticut refused to leave camp. Soon after moving out, Col. Le Caron drove up and informed me that the New York men were close at hand. I sent him back with orders to hurry them up at once. Our advance soon reached Alvah Richard's house, about twenty or thirty rods south of the line dividing Canada from the United States, and nearly half a mile from the enemy. Here I had the men, who were marching in column of fours, to halt, and after addressing a few words to the first company, numbering 32 men, under Capts. Cronin and Murphy, ordered them to advance as skirmishers, at the same time putting Col. John H. Brown, of Lawrence, Mass., in charge of the skirmish line. The enemy occupied a splendid position on the crest of a wooded hill, (Eccles Hill,) a little to the west of the road, which runs due north past Richards's house. On the American side, directly opposite the enemy, there was a corresponding wooded hill ; a small valley with a brook running through it, intervened. The bridge crossing the brook was about eight or ten rods from the line. The men were ordered by Col. Brown to deploy as skirmishers immediately after crossing it ; they might have been deployed before they got to the bridge, but the distance was so short and the ground not being advantageous, Col. Brown did not deem it necessary.

On the Canadian side of the line, for about four hundred yards, the ground is flat, and then rises abruptly into a steep rocky hill on which the enemy were posted—some of them behind large rocks nearer than was at first supposed. Just as the first of our men reached the bridge, the enemy opened a heavy fire on them. Almost at the first discharge, John Rowe, of Burlington, Vt., was shot through the heart, and fell dead on the centre of the road, and one other man was wounded. Only a few crossed the bridge. Our men returned the fire for a short time, but without effect, as the enemy were covered, and then scattered and sought shelter under the bridge, behind a fence, and a tannery close by. Some few came back to Richards's house. I remained at Richards's house with twenty-five men, with whom I intended supporting the skirmish line, but it fell back so suddenly there was no chance to support it. I had now ascertained all that I wanted, namely, that the enemy intended to defend the hill

I had no intention whatever of charging up it. If the men had been old soldiers, such men as I had at Ridgeway in 1866, I would have attempted a flank movement as soon as the skirmish line retreated ; but many of them were mere boys, who had never been in a fight before, and showed evident signs of wavering at the first fire of the enemy.

Soon after the firing commenced, I ordered the men in the rear across an open field, some one hundred and twenty-five yards up the hill to our left, which was covered with timber, and afforded an excellent shelter. While they were crossing the field, the enemy kept up a heavy fire on them, and killed one man, M. O'Brien of Moriah, N. Y., and wounded two others. The men had to cross a stone fence. On leaving the road, and in ascending the hill under the the enemy's fire, they were neither regular in their gait, precise in their step, nor did they keep a straight line, or observe the prescribed distance of "thirteen inches from breast to back." This was the only occasion in which there was any opportunity for the officers to display tactical knowledge, the absence of which has been so severely animadverted on by profound military critics, (profound asses,) not one of whom could handle a corporal's guard either on or off the field. As to lack of generalship, if there had been men to command, there would have been some opportunity for judging whether it was lacking or not ; as it was, there was not more than a captain's command present.

The large number of citizen spectators, who advanced with us, some of them ahead and some along side of the men, started for the rear as soon as the enemy commenced firing, and in doing so, created a good deal of confusion, which had a demoralizing effect on the men. Many of them had taken possession of the hill to our left, supposing they would have a good view and be perfectly safe from the enemy's bullets. Amongst them was a correspondent of the New York *Herald*, who made good time to the rear, leaving his horse behind. I left the men at Richards's house, in charge of Gen. Donnelly, and ascended the hill, on foot, under fire of the enemy. J. Boyle O'Riley, reporter for the Boston *Pilot*, did the same thing, under my instructions, a few moments previous.

As I ascended the hill, I noticed some of the men making for the rear, while those who remained were firing indiscriminately without judgment, and evidently doing the enemy no harm. When I got up the hill I tried to induce them to move forward to a more advantageous position, where they would have a fair view of the enemy, and be able to use their fire to some effect. But for the first time in my life I failed in rallying men or getting them to follow where I was willing to lead. J. Boyle O'Riley, Major Danl. Murphy, Capt. John Fitzpatrick, and other officers and men, whose names I do not know, acted very gallantly in trying to get the men forward, but with no result. Only a few were willing to venture forward. I fear that some of them had but a very imperfect idea of the duties incumbent upon them, or the responsibility they assumed, in swearing allegiance to the Irish Republican Army. They seemed to have a very erroneous idea as to the number of the enemy, (there were not a hundred of them, and volunteers at that,) which was confirmed to some extent by the rapidity of his fire. I believe he was armed with Spencer rifles ; I have been in many engagements, but never before heard so much firing where there was so little execution. Finding that I could not accomplish anything practical with these men, I had them to fall back a short distance out of range of the enemy's bullets, to await the arrival of the men from New York, under Col. Leddy, whom I looked for every moment. It was then I made the following remarks to the men :

"Men of Ireland I am ashamed of you! You have acted disgracefully to-day ; but you will have another chance of showing whether you are cravens or not. Comrades, we must not, we *dare* not go back with the stain of cowardice on us. Comrades, I will lead you again, and if you will not follow me, I will go with my officers and die in your front! I now leave you under charge of Boyle O'Riley, and will go after reinforcements, and bring them up at once."

I felt perfectly satisfied that when I got a few old soldiers up, particularly the men from New York, most of whom I knew personally, that they would do better. I have often seen men, when brought into action for the first time, act badly at the outset, but the moment reinforcements arrived they seemed to acquire new spirit and behave very gallantly. Fully one third of the men who ascended the hill, had fallen back, beyond the reach of my voice, before I got to the top. I started to bring them back, but seeing Gen. Foster, his deputy Failey, and others on the hill, in the direction in which they had fallen back, I returned. These men, who basely deserted their comrades, together with the few who refused to leave camp in the morning, were met on their way to St. Albans by newspaper reporters and others, and were the first to give circulation to the ridiculous stories of "want of judgment and military capacity," "bad generalship," etc., etc., which were so extensively circulated by the press of the country at the time. Of course these men were in the fight and saw it all. They took particular good care, however, not to remain very long. It was from these men that many of the newspaper reporters got the information which they sent to their respective papers, and which was published as " reliable news from their special correspondent on the field." The reporter for the New York *World*, who was near the field, was so gloriously drunk, that he and his note-book had to be picked up from the roadside that afternoon, by the sheriff of Chittenden County. No doubt his employers in New York believed that they were publishing a "correct report by an eye witness." I left my horse at Richards's house when I started to go up the hill. A gallant young man, named Timothy Sullivan, from Marlboro, Mass., volunteered to pass the open space through the enemy's fire and bring him back on the road so that I could ride to camp after the reinforcements; but on seeing the marshal close by, I did not go myself, but sent Col. Humphrey Sullivan, and instructed him to urge the men to hurry up as fast as possible. I had, previous to leaving Richards's house, sent Capt. John Lonergan, of Burlington, Vt., back after them. I subsequently saw the marshal go down to the road, and was informed that he had left for Franklin in his carriage; the carriage went back towards Franklin but he was not in it. In company with J. Boyle O'Riley, I examined the route for a flank movement from the position we were then occupying, and after waiting about an hour, fearing that we were giving the enemy too much time to get up his reinforcements, which I heard were not far off, I became impatient at the delay in the arrival of the men, and sent word to Gen. Donnelly by Col. Lewis, that I would go back and hurry them up, and would then make a flank movement to relieve him and the men at or near Richards's house. He would have been exposed to the fire of the enemy if he sought to change his position or fall back. On the return of Col. Lewis, informing the men that I was going back to hurry up reinforcements, (which seemed to please them very much,) I left them in charge of Major Danl. Murphy, and started with J. Boyle O'Riley down the hill, to the road leading to camp.

MY ARREST.

We struck the road, over half a mile from camp, at Mr. Vincent's house, in front of which lay one of our men wounded. A number of citizens were around him. We stopped a moment to speak with the wounded man, and, as we emerged from the crowd, General Foster, who had been concealed at the end of the house, approached me. We shook hands, and talked together for a moment. The following conversation, as near as I can recollect, took place:

Marshal.—"I think, General, you had better get in the carriage and drive back with me." (The carriage had just then returned.) I replied "No, I will not." He then spoke of his duty, and said "you are violating the neutrality laws." I replied that "I perfectly understood my position." He then said, "I am sorry, but I must arrest you, General O'Neill." I replied, "No, no, you must not, you cannot arrest me; I will not be arrested; I am armed, and will call on my men to assist me;" and tried to break away from the marshal and his deputy, Thomas Failey, both of whom got hold of me. He then said, "General O'Neill, I must arrest you, and I will; resistance is useless; I am also armed, and have more men than you have to assist me." The marshal, who saw me descend the hill, had made arrangements with the citizens to assist him. I looked around to see if any of my men were there to aid me in resisting arrest, but saw only one man, who had come back with the wounded man. I subsequently learned that there were two or three scattered amongst some fifty or sixty citizens. I was then over a quarter of a mile distant from any of my men, and more than half a mile from the camp. I had no arms but my sabre—my revolvers being in my saddle holsters. The citizens flocked around us. Seeing that further resistance was useless, I made none, and was assisted into the carriage by General Foster and his deputy, Thomas Failey. When I met General Foster, I was not certain whether he would attempt to arrest me or not, and when I thought of resisting, I was under the impression that several of my men were close by. On entering the carriage, I told the General "that he was assuming considerable responsibility." I then thought that we would meet the men on the march coming from camp, and that there might be some chance for them to stop the carriage and rescue me.

PASSING THROUGH CAMP.

The carriage was a light, close, two seated one, drawn by two powerful horses. General Foster sat in the back seat with me, while his deputy, Mr. Failey, sat in the front seat with the driver. The General cautioned me against giving any alarm, and kept his arm along the back part of the carriage, close by my neck, so as to prevent me from getting out or calling to the men in passing; but made no such threats as have been generally reported in the newspapers. The driver lashed the horses and drove furiously through the camp, past Colonel Leddy and his men. Some seem to think that, if I had given the alarm, the carriage could have been stopped and myself rescued; but this I do not believe, although I was of that opinion myself when arrested. To have stopped the carriage, under the circumstances, would have required more nerve and judgment than most of men possess. Had the officer in charge known of my arrest before we got up, and had he posted two or three men on the road, away from the others, they might have shot one or both of the horses while passing. Even this is doubtful, as the horses were going very rapidly. Or if he had placed a few men at a charge bayonets across the road, and if they had stood their ground, which is very doubtful, they could stop the carriage. He might also have blocked the road with boxes, barrels, etc. I do not believe that there was a single officer there who would have ordered an indiscriminate firing at the horses from either side of the road while the men were scattered on both sides of it. To have caught the horses at the rate they were going, and stopped them, was simply out of the question. But, as the officers and men knew nothing of my arrest, before I could give the alarm and have it understood, with the rattling of the carriage, and the noise and confusion amongst the men themselves, I would have been borne out of reach. The deputy marshal and driver, sitting in front of the carriage, as soon as they came up to the men, commenced calling out at the top of their voice, "Clear the way! Clear the way!" which was done instantly, and a free passage made—the carriage not having to relax its speed even for a second. Hence any effort I might have made to make my situation intelligible, could not be acted upon in time to effect my release. The fact that there were 150 or more men in camp did not mend the matter. Half a dozen of men would have been infinitely better. Numbers in such a case only tend to confuse. That General Foster was prepared to prevent any alarm being given, or any conversation between myself and the men, so far as physical strength would enable him to prevent it—and he is a large and powerful man—I am fully aware of, from the position he occupied in the carriage. That he would have resorted to the use of fire-arms, except in self-defence, I do not believe; and while I very much regret being arrested at such a time, and would not have permitted it if I could have avoided it, yet I have no fault to find with General Foster for performing a duty which he was sworn to discharge, and only regret that chance enabled him to perform it. At the time, I did not regret my arrest so much, because I knew that the command would devolve on General J. J. Donnelly, who was cognizant of nearly all my plans. The unfortunate accident he met with, in escaping from the position he occupied at Richards's house, (from which I had hoped soon to relieve him,) caused me to bitterly regret the unfortunate circumstance that lodged me in a jail. After my arrest, I had no opportunity of communicating with the command either at Franklin or Malone.

PRECAUTIONS AGAINST ARREST.

With the fate of Gen. Sweeney, who was arrested at his hotel in St. Albans, during the movement of 1866, before me, I had determined on taking every precaution that I possibly could against a similar mischance. On Saturday morning, the 21st inst., I left Buffalo, N. Y., and arrived in Troy the same evening, avoiding, as much as possible, seeing any person in Troy. I took the sleeping car and arrived at Georgia Depot, Vermont, early the next morning, (Sunday,) where a friend met me with his buggy and took me to his house in the country. Here I remained all day Sunday and Monday, and put on a disguise suit, which had been purchased for me by a friend in Buffalo. At 2 o'clock Tuesday morning, this gentleman took me in his buggy to St. Albans, where we arrived at the house of a friend a little after daylight. My principal business at St. Albans was to see Gen. Donnelly, and to give him final instructions previous to his starting for St. Johns, but through the failure of the men to arrive, this part of the programme had to be abandoned, and I started with the same friend who had brought me to St. Albans, for Franklin, as before stated. Up to my arrival at Franklin there were not more than half a dozen men (and they all perfectly reliable) in that section of country, who knew anything about my whereabouts. At Franklin, from the number of orders and instructions I was obliged to give, crowds of citizens met me at every turn. I found that I was soon recognized, but there was no marshal in the vicinity at the time; besides I was in the midst of my men and would not have submitted to arrest. I claim, therefore, to have taken every precaution that it was possible for me to take to avoid arrest. No doubt there are very many who can now see clearly, and without spectacles, how easily I could have avoided arrest, or been rescued after my arrest, but they were not in my place, and I question very much if they would have done any better if they had been. Talk is cheap.

COMMITMENT TO PRISON.

General Foster, whose conduct throughout has been that of a gentleman, drove me rapidly to St. Albans, where I was brought before United States Commissioner Smalley, on a charge of having violated the neutrality laws. I waived examination, and in default of twenty thousand dollars bail, was committed to jail at Burlington, where I arrived the same evening, and where, to the credit of the Fenian Brotherhood, I still remain.

LETTER FROM GENERAL GEORGE P. FOSTER, UNITED STATES MARSHAL, ON THE ARREST.

WINDSOR, VT., October 13, 1870.

GENERAL JOHN O'NEILL :

SIR : I have read your statement in regard to your arrest, and the circumstances connected with it, at Franklin, Vt., on the 25th day of May, 1870, and unhesitatingly concur with you in regard to what transpired at that time.

GEO. P. FOSTER, U. S. Marshal.

The following letter from reporters of the press, who were in camp before we left, went out with us and were at Richards's house during the skirmish, (one of them, J. Boyle O'Riley, was with me from the time I ascended the hill until my arrest,) although intended by them as private, and so regarded by me, yet I take the liberty of publishing it. (I hope the gentlemen will pardon the liberty.) It is from parties whose opportunities for forming a correct opinion were certainly as good as those of reporters who remained at St. Albans, gathering their information from men who ran away, and drawing inspiration from Canadian whiskey, which no doubt was furnished duty free.

ST. ALBANS, VT., Morning of the 26th May, 1870.

GENERAL JOHN O'NEILL :

MY DEAR GENERAL : As you ordered me, I told my command on the hill that you had been arrested. I then gave the command to Major Daniel Murphy, of Bridgeport, Conn. He determined to fall back to the place where the stores lay. Whilst forming his command, Captain Griffin, from New York, arrived and reported a reinforcement, in the rear, of 150 men. I then went down to General Donnelly. He was deeply affected when I told him of your arrest. He could not leave his place, but determined to do so in the night. He did so last night, and is now with the main body at the stores. The United States troops have arrived here. I am going to the front with the *other reporters*. In their names I can assure you that you need not fear that your name will sustain one iota of blemish. It is in our hands, and we know the truth and will promulgate it.

Always yours, respectfully,

J. BOYLE O'REILLY, Boston Pilot.
H. S. HART, Burlington Free Press.
M. B. CARPENTER, Troy Press.
H. S. TUTTLE, Rutland Herald.
C. H. TUTTLE, Boston Advertiser.

The reports furnished by these gentlemen to their respective papers were in the main correct.

MY ARREST A FORTUNATE CIRCUMSTANCE.

Previous to leaving camp I was under the impression, derived from the best sources of information at my command, that there were about four hundred men on the road from St. Albans, who were expected every moment, and over a thousand men who had arrived at St. Albans on the morning train, and who would get to us during the day. If the Fenians of New York and Brooklyn, on whom I depended at the last moment, instead of counting their *dollars* as *diamonds*, when dealing with a man who had before and was again willing to risk; and if necessary to sacrifice, that which all the dollars of all of them combined could not purchase, his life, and instead of indulging in their doubts and fears as to whether there was going to be a movement or not, had furnished me with a few hundred dollars for contingent expenses, which I had asked of them previous to leaving the city, and which they had promised me, I would have been in a position to have bought horses which would have enabled me to have got more correct information. But they were much more exacting in the promises that I made to them than they were in redeeming their own, on which mine to a great extent were based. As it was, I had neither horses nor money, and had to depend almost entirely on the reports brought me by outsiders. It would now appear that these reports were very much exaggerated, and that only between six and seven hundred men altogether arrived at St. Albans during the excitement. With this fact before me, I have no hesitation in saying, that it was a very fortunate circumstance that I had been arrested at the time I was, for if I had not been, I certainly would have crossed the line, believing that large reinforcements would immediately join us, and in all probability much bloodshed, without any permanent good to the cause of Ireland, would have been the result; and however anxious I might have been to vindicate my own character by having a fight, I would certainly have regretted being the cause of shedding blood where no good could result from it.

AFTER MY ARREST.

After I had been arrested, no practical effort was made by the men from New York, or any others, to cross the line or advance to the front to relieve General Donnelly—a man whom most of them knew personally, and one who, when in New York a short time previous, had received the assurance from them, that they had every confidence in him, and desired him for their commanding officer. Why this was so is more than I am able to say. There were several officers amongst them who had seen service, and, certainly, the air of confidence and self-complacency with which some of them criticised and condemned myself and others for want of judgment and military capacity, (I don't know that they have got through talking yet,) would lead one to believe that they would use a little of that profound wisdom and military capacity, which made them such excellent fault-finders, in attempting a flank movement or doing something to create a diversion in favor of General Donnelly, so that he might be enabled to get out of his dangerous position without having the whole of the enemy's fire concentrated upon him. I presume, however, that these wiseacres found it much easier to censure others than do better themselves.

Major Murphy abandoned the hill during the afternoon, which left the enemy free to devote special attention to Gen. Donnelly, and the few men he had at Richards's house. Gen. Donnelly and most of his men effected their escape before dark. In order to convey a more intelligent idea of what transpired after my arrest, I shall publish the reports of the officers who were present.

The following named officers deserve special mention for gallantry displayed during the skirmish:—Gen. J. J. Donnelly, Col. John H. Brown, Capt. Charles

Carlton, A. D. C., Major Daniel Murphy, Capts. Wm. Cronin, Thos. Murphy, John Fitzpatrick, and Lieut. John Hallaghan. Also Capt. Ahern, of Connecticut, and the officers mentioned in Major Murphy's Report. Capt. Carlton and Lieut. Hallaghan were wounded.

CAUSE OF THE FAILURE.

It is very evident from the foregoing that the cause of the failure is to be attributed to the want of men. Now why is this? Why is it that men who love their native land as Irishmen do, and who are always sighing for a chance to fight, and if necessary die to serve that land, were not on hand to take advantage of the opportunity when it presented itself? For this a variety of reasons may be given, but the following is perhaps the strongest:

The people, so often deceived and disappointed in the past, could not believe that we were in earnest, and thousands of good men who were anxious to be with us, kept indulging their doubts and fears until too late to be of service. As a general thing, the best men did not leave their homes until after the movement had commenced. The Senate party had their emissaries at work all over the country, destroying the confidence of the people. Amongst this number, one of the meanest and most unprincipled was a Lieut. Wm. E. Dougherty, of the 1st U. S. Infantry. This man, who, from his position in the regular army, one might expect to be a gentleman, occasionally parades his self-importance and abuse of others in the columns of that respectable vehicle of enlightenment, the *Irish Republic.* The honorable and high-toned editor of this sheet frequently indulges in slandering men in one issue to beg their pardon in the next. The lieutenant, in the exuberance of his patriotism, and from a great anxiety to serve the cause, in the summer of 1868, offered his services to the Organization to make a tour of observation through Canada, (a pleasure excursion); and, notwithstanding the fact that he drew his salary as an officer of the United States Army, during the time, charged the Organization the very modest sum of $1,225.00 for his services. From the vast amount of information obtained, which must be of more service to himself than anybody else, he prepared several plans for the invasion of Canada, such as the merest tyro in the art of war might prepare for an organization having a government at its back with gunboats, transports, artillery, etc., but which no one but an empty egotist would think of preparing for the Fenian Organization. The plans, however, were voluminous, and were no doubt highly edifying to the profound statesmen and would be soldiers of the Senate.

WHO IS RESPONSIBLE FOR THE ATTEMPT AT THE "INVASION OF CANADA?"

While I do not wish to shield myself from the responsibility attached to any act of mine, as a member of the Fenian Organization, or its President, yet, I repeat it, that I had nothing to do with originating the scheme of freeing Ireland through an invasion of Canada. Some of those who originated it have done much to bring about the failure. It was the policy of the Organization before I became a member; it continued to be its policy after the abortive attempt of 1866. The five last annual Congresses of the Brotherhood endorsed this policy, and declared their determination to carry it out. At every meeting of the Senate, since the split in the organization in 1865, that body passed resolutions declaring their unalterable determination to carry out that policy Should they now try to excuse themselves, it can only be on the plea of previous insincerity, which plea I am willing to accept. The representatives of the Organization in eighteen States of the Union, in their State Conventions which I attended, endorsed this policy and pledged themselves to furnish the means necessary to its prosecution. It was on this policy and for the purpose of assisting in carrying it out, that I accepted the position of President of the Organization in January, 1868. I believed in the policy, and for nearly two years and a half have been its special representative, advocating it all over the country. The people who knew that I represented the expressed wishes of the Organization, put faith in what I said, because they saw me to be earnest, and knew that I had given practical evidence of my earnestness at the head of the men who crossed the Niagara in 1866, and fought at "Ridgeway." I am of opinion that thousands joined the Organization on my account, and that thousands who were in it, would have left it long ago, did they not believe that I intended to fight.

Had it not been for the oft-repeated declarations and assurances that we purposed to fight in Canada, and that soon, the Organization could not have been kept together; for there was another Fenian Organization, presided over by Mr. John Savage, which strongly opposed ours, and had always adhered to the policy of fighting in Ireland. The only difference or cause for disunion between the rank and file of the two organizations, was the difference in policy. Some of the leaders, doubtless, were actuated by personal motives in perpetuating disunion.

Besides this, there were other organizations, some of them secret, whose object also was to assist the men at home. But all of them, I am perfectly satisfied, would have helped us if we had made a successful beginning. I have therefore been simply the agent in carrying out the oft-repeated policy of the Fenian Brotherhood. If others were not in earnest, I was. I never made a promise or a pledge to the people which I have not tried to make good. The people, through their representatives, have made pledges to me which they have not redeemed. I think that the system of misrepresentation practiced by some of our Irish patriots, has done more to injure the cause and destroy the confidence of the people than a dozen of defeats on the field. The particular time for inaugurating the movement being controlled by the circumstances heretofore related, I am responsible for nothing more. If I had not commenced the movement at the time I did, others, both in the East and in the West, would have made the attempt.

"SHALL ANOTHER ATTEMPT BE MADE TO INVADE CANADA?"

Is a question which I have been asked frequently since my imprisonment; to which I answer, No! emphatically no. And now I give timely notice to any man or set of men who may have any idea of attempting it again, while England and Canada are at peace with the world, that nothing that it is possible for me to do shall be left undone to frustrate it. Believing that the only opportunity for success in that direction has passed, and passed forever, I shall for the future be found as zealous in my opposition to such an enterprise as I have been hitherto earnest, laborious, and persevering in its advocacy. In all candor and sincerity I advise those who have heretofore or do now believe in freeing Ireland through an invasion of Canada, while England and Canada are at peace with the world, to abandon the idea at once. With the United States authorities to hold you back on one side, and the vigilance and forward state of preparations (continually on the increase) of the Canadian authorities to meet you on the other, you will never be able to get a sufficient number of men with arms and ammunition across the border in time to take up a position which can be held.

You will be told by that venerable patriot, James Gibbons, of Philadelphia, who signs himself "Chairman Executive Council, F. B.," and who is simply the tool and mouthpiece of another, that this is the advice of one who has himself failed because he assumed powers not delegated to him by the Organization; because he undertook a movement on his own responsibility and without the sanction of the people. By the people, in this case, are meant James Gibbons and P. J. Meehan. It has taken this man and his associates a long time to find out that I was not to be trusted, and that henceforth you must look to him, as the head of a body, calling itself the Executive Council of the F. B., for Irish freedom. According to him, said body only possesses the right to speak for the Irish Nationalists of America, and anything done or said for Irish liberty, must first be sanctioned by it to be legitimate. Believe him not; this man, with his confreres, after doing all they could to break up the Organization and destroy the confidence of the people, was elected by a fraction of the Fenian Brotherhood, at Chicago, Ill., in April last. He had previously been Vice President of the Fenian Brotherhood, and, until a very recent period, was one of the most earnest advocates of the very movement which he and his associates afterwards did so much to defeat. In his better days he condemned in the strongest language, the men who were standing in the way of a successful invasion of Canada; even P. J. Meehan came in for a large share of his censure. But, being a man of no stability of character, though his pretensions on that point are very considerable, he is completely at the mercy of every designing knave who chooses to humor his vanity for corrupt purposes.

They will now try to build up an Organization under the pretence of preparing for an immediate fight for Irish liberty. But I am inclined to the opinion that their powers for disorganization and demoralization, which were recently used to such good effect, are much greater than their powers for reorganizing and re-establishing confidence. But if they can succeed in getting up even a nominal Organization, they will proclaim to the world through that veracious journal, the "*Irish American*," and one or two lesser lights, that they only are the representatives of the Irish Nationalists of America, and must have a few *fat offices*—with a little *Corporation printing*—for themselves and their friends; this, of course, by way of hastening the day of Irish independence. They will tell you that the unauthorized attempt of the President of the Fenian Brotherhood to carry out the sole mission of the Organization "cannot be recognized as a defeat"—certainly not—"and that the work must go on." If this delusion can only be kept up until the next Presidential election, all will be well. The only representatives of the Irish National Organization know how to take care of themselves.

WHAT SHALL BE DONE WITH THE ARMS AND WAR MATERIAL OF THE F. B.

I would advise that the United States Government retain what they have of them for a short time. To turn them over to the only Organization that would be likely to make such a claim at present, would be simply to assist in building up a political structure for the elevation of a few individuals. Circles or persons having arms, etc., of the F. B. in their possession, would do well to hold on to them until a union of the F. B. is completed.

A WORD WITH OUR CANADIAN FRIENDS.

I have heretofore referred to you, as enemies. I could not speak of men whom I desired to fight in any other way. Our only object was to make war on England—a nation with which we have been at perpetual war for the last seven hundred years, and shall so continue to be as long as she claims the right to misgovern Ireland. You recognize the English government as your government, and the English flag as your flag. We desired to destroy both. You were ready to defend both; hence our only cause of quarrel with you. If we had been able, we would not have hesitated to kill every soldier who was ready to fight for England. The majority of us were in earnest, although a few designing knaves and political tricksters succeeded in demoralizing the Brotherhood at a critical moment. If we had not been in earnest, the large amount of arms and war material which many of you saw on the border, and the large amount which you did not see, but which was not far off, (enough for over twenty thousand men, and costing hundreds of thousands of dollars,) would not have been found in our possession. That we would have inflicted many of the evils consequent upon a state of warfare, cannot be denied. That we would have permitted murder, robbery, etc., or that we had any intention of appropriating any of your property or lands, or that such was any part of our object, I deny emphatically, and refer you for proof of this assertion to the movement in '66, and to the conduct of our men when hundreds of them were on your soil for two days, opposite Buffalo. I now of course speak of the men under my command. No doubt some of those who came to the border during both movements came there to indulge their natural propensities for pillaging; but had we succeeded on the other side, these men would soon be given to understand that their wishes were not in harmony with the mission of the Fenian Brotherhood. That you are now both able and willing to protect yourselves against any further attempts on our part to annoy you, I am fully satisfied. I speak for the men who were in earnest in this matter, and assure you that you shall have no further annoyance from us. That we have been a source of trouble and expense to you for nearly five years I need not tell you; but your trouble is now at an end. We had a very different object in view from keeping you in alarm. The men amongst us who intended to fight will now take care of the *talking patriots*, who would buy a cheap notoriety by keeping up the appearance of preparing for a fight which it is their intent shall never come off. In a word, we will put an end to the humbug of a "Fenian invasion of Canada," at least as long as you keep out of difficulty at home and abroad. You are satisfied with the English government, and that the English flag should float over, I will not say, protect, you; that is henceforth your business, not ours. There are many of our countrymen amongst you, happy and contented, who no doubt were bitterly opposed to our plan of freeing Ireland, while some others might entertain a different opinion. We now desire to live at peace with you and them, and when you commence housekeeping on your own account, if you should send us a pressing invitation, we will be pleased to visit you, or, if you should prefer to join the great family of Uncle Sam, we will be delighted to receive and recognize you as brothers. As for the trouble and expense we have been to you of late, what have you actually lost? Nothing. Look at your condition from a military stand-point five years ago and look at it now. I repeat it, you have lost nothing; and I would respectfully suggest that you place on the credit side of that little account on your ledger of five million of dollars, which the newspapers say you are going to present to Uncle Sam as indemnity for losses sustained in resisting Fenian invasions, twenty millions gained in military prestige, you will still have fifteen millions to your credit. This proceeding will be much more sensible than to prove your ingratitude to Uncle Sam by presenting the above bill; for he has been a good friend of yours on two occasions within the recollection of the present generation.

CONCLUSION.

Nearly five years ago I joined the Fenian Brotherhood with the simple wish of serving the cause of Irish liberty. Soon after, I was called upon to abandon home, family and business to fight for Ireland. My business, at the time, was extensive, worth to me at least fifty thousand dollars, which the years and energy since devoted by me to Fenianism would have more than doubled. I hesitated not a moment to risk all. Accident put me in command of the men who fought at Ridgeway. This fight was a success, though the movement proved a failure. You cheered and applauded; proclaimed me a hero, a great patriot, skillful commander, etc.; expressed a wish to see me and hear me, that you might shower your congratulations upon me. I sought nothing so much as to go home and resume the care of my business, feeling that I had simply done my duty to Ireland, as far as in my power. On reaching home, I found my affairs in a ruinous condition, and saw the necessity of giving them my whole and immediate attention. In the meantime, letters from the circles of the Organization, inviting me to visit them, poured in upon me from all quarters from a grateful people—so they said—who desired to show their appreciation of the distinguished services rendered by me to the Brotherhood and the cause of Ireland. I accepted as few of these invitations as possible, and attended to my business, satisfied that my services as a patriot in travelling through the country, making speeches, etc., would be none the less appreciated, if I could afford to pay my own expenses. I did not then know how skillfully those two pure and disinterested patriots and Christian gentlemen, P. J. Meehan and James Gibbons, could torture legitimate travelling expenses—railroad fare, hotel bills, etc., incurred in carrying out their own resolutions—into "squandering the hard-earned money of our people." I had heard, however, some mean talk about paid officials and men living upon the Organization, just as if men of ability, depending on their own exertions for a livelihood, could devote their time and talents to the Organization gratuitously. Had they turned the Organization into a means of procuring fat political positions for themselves, as more than one unpaid official has done, then they could have well afforded to give their services to the Brotherhood without other compensation. My desire was to put myself in a position to *serve* Ireland, when the opportunity arose, without requiring any remuneration whatever for my services.

But it would seem that this was not to be. For the second time, at a critical moment, when absence from business would involve a certain loss of thousands of dollars, (having just paid out six thousand dollars to a lawyer in Washington to get control again of my business there,) I was called upon by Mr. Meehan and others, not to fight immediately, but to first save the Organization by accepting the Presidency. Mr. Meehan has since informed me that, if I had then refused the presidency, the Organization would have gone to pieces—but others are as competent to judge of the matter as he. I am now of opinion that Colonel Roberts retained the office as long as he thought there was any chance of accomplishing any good, and then insisted on resigning. Mr. Gibbons reluctantly consented to the arrangement by which I became president, as he coveted the position for himself; he had then, as on all other occasions, to yield to the wishes of Meehan. I might here add that the honor of being President of the Fenian Brotherhood—at a time when the failure of the "union negotiations" and the resignation of Colonel Roberts had completely demoralized the Brotherhood—had no peculiar charms for me, and could not raise me in the eyes of our people. On the contrary, had I, after the fashion of Irish patriots, retired on the glories of the past, on the laurels of Ridgeway, I might have sought and obtained a political position for myself, and become a great hero and patriot for the balance of my natural life, having Meehan, Gibbons, Carey and all the rest of them, to herald my praises from Maine to California. How foolish some men are!

Nothing but the prospect of a brush with the enemy that year could have justified me in thus for the second time abandoning my business and my creditors. I did not then know that I was simply intended by that arch-hypocrite, Meehan, as a tool to be used by him so long as I was found useful and pliant, and afterward to be thrown aside, as others had been before me. He is a good mechanic, and will take all necessary pains to sharpen his tools; but, woe unto them, if they fail to perform their allotted work! The columns of the *Irish American* will suddenly change colors, and the character that, yesterday, was white as the driven snow, will, to-day, stand forth black as Erebus. Should the case prove a difficult one, that gray-haired patriot, Gibbons, who is too much of a Christian to lie on his own account, but never yet refused to do it for his master, will be called upon for assistance.

In compliance with the Senate resolutions, I labored night and day for nearly two years to prepare the Organization for action. The men who induced me to accept the presidency had other engagements to occupy their time and thoughts. They could pass resolutions of a warlike character periodically, but at the same time be extremely careful to avoid taking warlike measures. If resolutions could give liberty to a people, the Senate of the F. B. would long ago have made Ireland the freest nation on the globe. They will now account to you for their inaction by the statement that they had no intention to strike until the opportune moment arrived; they should have so informed us at the start, but they preferred feeding you with false promises, and getting me, through their high-blown resolutions, to do the same. They will also tell you, that we were not prepared for a fight. No; and what is more, we never should, so long as it was in their power to prevent it. I believe we were as well prepared for a fight in Canada this spring as we might ever hope to be; for the people were grown sick and tired of our oft-repeated and as often broken promises; they were in no humor to sustain the Organization any longer as it stood: we must either fight or boldly declare a change of policy. The Senate, or rather P. J. Meehan, for it is useless to allude to the majority of that body except as his tool, would do neither the one nor the other. No! the delusion must be kept up, and a plausible excuse for delaying the fight invented—a quarrel with the President would serve this purpose best.

"O'Neill assisted us for a time, but he now wants to redeem the pledges made to the people in our name. He must be disposed of, as no longer a pliant tool. His character has to be ruined, and we are experts in the business. John O'Neill is become a second John O'Mahoney, and No. 10 W. Fourth St., a Moffat Mansion. We, the representatives of the people, fifteen in number, no matter if there is only a quorum of eight, with the *Irish American*, *United Irishman*, and *Irish Republic* at our back, can make short work of him. Some, who may happen to know better, will not believe us, but the masses who know nothing of the facts in the case, will take the word of fifteen men before that of one man, especially as they form a delegated body authorized to speak for the Organization. Carey, McCloud, Hynes, Gibbons, Dunne, Fitzgerald, and McKinley, are thoroughly conversant with their parts. Taking our experience into consideration, failure is impossible. Our work, indeed, is not very honorable, but that matters not; have we not fought John O'Mahony and can we not fight any other man? Some of our number are rather too scrupulous to co-operate, but they are not many, and will not offer much active opposition, while we have such resources for defamation at our disposal. In the end, they, too, will have to fall into line, [some of them, however, to their credit, disappointed this expectation]. If we could only force a quarrel with O'Neill; but it is now evident that we must begin it ourselves, since, in spite of repeated provocations, he keeps his temper. Quarrel, however, we must, at all hazards. We have placed ourselves on record in favor of a fight; that fact we will publish to the world, but, just as we are almost ready to meet the enemy, we will have to stop, in order to save the honor of the Irish race, and the very Organization, from ruin. Happy thought! it will work like a charm. It will furnish us with a sufficient pretext for deferring a fight for the next half century. Should he, however, attempt to fight without our permission, [which will never be given,] we will see to it that the movement is a failure, and we have done much towards that already in destroying public confidence. We will then throw the whole blame on him, and proclaim to the world our own wisdom and forethought in seeing disaster ahead. We are the only representatives of the Irish people, and we only have the right to order a fight for Ireland."

God help poor Ireland, if she has to remain in bondage until freed by such men!

Let it not be supposed that I have any idea that the co-operation of the Senate at the time of the movement would have enabled us to succeed, for I have not. The one great essential to success, apart from a supply of arms, was a sufficient number of men with faith and confidence enough in the leaders to inaugurate the movement and transport the war material across the line before either government could know of their designs. In this lay the great difficulty. Once the movement was fairly set on foot, no man or set of men, no matter what their pretensions, could keep Irishmen from fighting for their country. Hence the start was everything. The Senate, through its false promises and resolutions during the last two years, had so often deceived the people that nearly all confidence was lost in that honorable body, and since I, as President, was the principal representative of the Senate, many who at first had all faith in my honesty of purpose, began to have serious misgivings of my sincerity. I at no time, however, made a promise to the people which was not made in perfect good faith, and to be carried out at the risk of my life.

In 1866 the Senate, in spite of the fact that thousands of soldiers, both Irish and American, just returned from the battle-fields of a great civil war, were ready to embark in any enterprise of the kind, and that their chief military officer was Gen. T. W. Sweeny, one of the most popular soldiers of the Irish race, were unable, after making the greatest exertions, to place more men on the border within three days after commencing to move, than we did within the same period. It was not until after the fight at Ridgeway that the people began to put faith in the enterprise, and that men flocked to the border. Had the fight at Eccles Hill gone on—it had hardly commenced when I was arrested—and been a second "Ridgeway," and had we remained, as in 1866, two days on the other side, I have no doubt that there would have been a greater rush to the border than occurred in 1866. That they would have come too late to be of any practical service, I also believe; for after the first few days the enemy was well prepared, and the United States Government ready to intercept us. In 1866 the entire blame of the failure fell on the shoulders of Gen. Sweeny; in 1870, Gen. O'Neill is the only one censured. In 1866 James Stephens denounced the movement as treason to Ireland; in 1870 James Gibbons begins where Stephens left off. So it goes. I do not know whether Gibbons went to Washington and dined with the Secretary of State, and in the evening had himself serenaded, and made a speech from the balcony at Willard's, denouncing the movement, or not—all of which Stephens is said to have done—but he issued a proclamation which will be read by posterity, and which no doubt pleased him quite as well.

In 1866, people generally supposed, myself among the number, that our movement was nipped in the bud by the United States Government, but, such was not the case. On the contrary, we had opportunities afforded us such as we could not again hope for. The most that we could safely calculate upon before the direct interference of the U. S. Government, was three days, and all of that time was allowed us. With a position secured on the other side, men would afterwards join us despite the vigilance of the Government. My own arrest by Gen. Foster was purely accidental. He had no soldiers to assist him in stopping the movement. I have no fault, therefore, to find with the action of the Government; for, while it is its bounden duty to preserve the neutrality laws, when it is evident that they are in danger of infringement, we had every reasonable opportunity for evading the Government. The failure of the movement is rather due to the failure of our men to come up in time.

The earnest co-operation of the Senate could not have improved our chances of success, since both Governments would have been prepared to stop us at the very start, as they would long beforehand have been apprised of our design. It would be impossible for that body to keep such a secret. At one of their meetings, held in Pittsburgh, Pa., June 29th, 1869, it was determined, in secret session, to commence a movement on the 15th of the following September. The first I knew of their having fixed the date was gleaned from the columns of a Canadian newspaper. The sincerity, however, of this, their resolution, may be judged from the fact that, before adjourning, they pledged themselves, each to go to work in his respective locality from the date of their return home until the 10th of August, when they were to reassemble in New York to make final arrangements, and there remain until the outset of the movement. This solemn pledge to work actively for the cause was broken by nearly all of them. A few of them came to New York at the appointed time, but it was not until after the lapse of a week or ten days that they were able to have a quorum; and when they did meet, they had other matters beside the preparations for a fight with the enemy to occupy their time. A quarrel with the President was found much more congenial to their tastes. It is needless to say that they did not remain in session until the army of the F. B. took the field.

Now, however, the long desired period for loud talk and patriotic inactivity has arrived. They can now safely pass warlike resolutions and issue addresses to their hearts' content. Nobody for the future will be so fool-hardy as to insist upon a practical compliance with their promises, and the farce will be permitted to go on without interruption. Gibbons may now play without fear of rebuke his humorous role of military critic and instructor. Poor old man! the martial spirit still predominates; let it have vent—the display will give him pleasure and harm no one.

But why should I speak? I, the inmate of a common jail," "the associate of thieves, house-burners, and every class of disreputable characters;" an "object of pity and contempt," and the "laughing-stock of all!" Perhaps so. I still, however, claim the right to speak, as one who joined the Fenian Brotherhood to the direct injury of his every personal interest, in the hope of serving Ireland; as one who, with others, risked his life for Ireland under circumstances when few would have ventured, and, in so doing, won for the Brotherhood the only victory it ever achieved on the field; as one who, for the last eighteen months, suffered untold tortures sooner than have an open rupture with men who falsely professed to be working with him for Ireland; as one who robbed his family and his friends (his creditors) of the time and labor which properly belonged to them, and who, with half of the energy devoted to his business which he devoted to the cause, would have, at least, a home and the comforts of life for his wife and children during his enforced absence in prison, instead of leaving them entirely destitute, without a dollar to pay the grocery bill or the month's rent. I still claim the right to speak, as one accused of squandering the hard-earned money of our people by the very parties who induced him by their false promises to abandon his only means of support—his private business, and who was afterwards compelled to deprive his family even of the necessaries of life, in order to meet his obligations, and who has now lain for several weeks in prison without a dollar to fee a lawyer, and with the prospect of being immured within its walls for an indefinite period. I claim the privilege to speak, as one who defies the most malignant, lying scoundrel among his accusers to point to a *single* dollar of Fenian money by him squandered or misappropriated. In spite of the charges to the contrary, made by the

IMMACULATE Senators, Gibbons, Dunne, Hynes and McCloud, at the Chicago Convention, I shall be able to prove the honesty of my dealings with the Organization from their own evidence in the general statement of my connection with the Fenian Brotherhood, soon to be published.

To the question, "What is become of the moneys paid into the Fenian Treasury?" the best answer is contained in the following interrogatory: "How were all the arms, war material and clothing, which thousands saw at Franklin and Malone, procured and transported to the border?" The alteration of breech-loaders alone cost, according to Mr. Meehan, over sixty thousand dollars; and the Organization is in possession of ammunition and war material besides that collected at Malone and Franklin.

In some few instances where I attended the meetings of circles, or accompanied special committees appointed to collect funds in Brooklyn and New York, the money was given to me to be turned into the treasury. The Treasurer's books and the financial statements will show that such moneys were in every instance handed into the treasury, and the circles properly credited therewith. The only money of the Fenian Brotherhood with which I have had anything to do, from the time I became President, in January, 1868, up to the Congress held in New York, last April, was that allowed me for salary and travelling expenses; the vouchers for which were examined and approved by the representatives of the Organization at the Congresses held in Philadelphia and New York. One of my chief defamers, at present, James Gibbons, was a party to their examination and approval. My travelling expenses were heavy, because I travelled a great deal at the urgent desire of the Senate, to further the interests of the Organization. For every dollar I have received since the adjournment of the New York Congress I am prepared to furnish the necessary vouchers.

Nothing but the *mean, lying, cowardly,* attacks made upon my character, both privately and publicly, in connection with the funds of the Organization, could justify me, in referring to my business or family affairs in this statement. The task is not a pleasant one, but it has been forced upon me by unprincipled assailants.

Finally, I claim the privilege to speak, as one who (notwithstanding the unjust and false reports of newspapers and newspaper correspondents, including "Druid" (James Brennan) of the *Irish American*, the meanest and most cowardly liar of them all—a man who, in the past, talked loudly and learnedly of war, but who managed to keep at a safe distance during the danger, and who afterwards came to survey the situation, and, jackal-like, pilfer the character of true men,) as one I say, who has materially aided in preparing the Irish people to strike a blow at England, such as she had not received for ages. It will be long, I fear, before Irishmen have another such opportunity, and, that the one just past was not taken advantage of, they have but their own supineness to blame.

To that portion of the Fenian Brotherhood, having for its object the freedom of Ireland through an invasion of Canada, I now bid farewell, and hereby resign all connection, official or otherwise, with it. I was an Irishman, a patriot, and a soldier for Ireland, before I ever had the honor of being enrolled a Fenian. I am all three still. My connection with the Organization has neither made me a "coward," a "traitor to Ireland," nor a "dishonest man."

I remain, gentlemen,

Very respectfully, your ob't servant,

JOHN O'NEILL.

OFFICIAL REPORT

OF THE

BATTLE OF RIDGEWAY, CANADA WEST,

FOUGHT JUNE 2d. 1866.

HEADQUARTERS, LAKE ERIE DEP'T, I. R. A.,
June 27th, 1866.

BRIG. GENL. C. C. TEVIS, Adjt. Genl. I. R. A.

General:—The following is an official report of the action of the men under my command, from the time I left Nashville, Tenn., May 27th, 1866, until June 3d, 1866:

In obedience to orders received from you, while I was in New York, I left Nashville, May 27th, 1866, with one hundred and fifteen (115) men. On arriving at Louisville, Ky., Col. Owen Starr, in command of one hundred and forty-four (144) men joined us; and at Indianapolis we were joined by about one hundred (100) men under the command of Capt. Haggerty. We all arrived at Cleveland, Ohio, on the night of the 28th ult., where I supposed we would attempt to cross the lake. But no orders to that effect had been received there; nor any person there that could give us any definite information on the subject.

During the day of the 29th, Senator Morrison arrived from New York with orders and instructions from General Sweeny, for Brig. Gen. Lynch. In the absence of Gen. Lynch, the senior officer present was to receive the orders, and carry out the instructions, which were: to effect a crossing at that point. It was at once decided that Col. Owen Starr should command the expedition. But during that afternoon Senator Bannon received a telegram from General Sweeny, in answer to one which he sent in the morning, directing the men assembled at Cleveland, to proceed at once to Buffalo, where Capt. Hynes, his Asst. Adjt. Genl., had been sent with instructions and orders.

We arrived in Buffalo on the morning of the 30th, and reported to Capt. Hynes. Here the men were distributed in squads all over the city.

I was informed by Capt. Hynes, that he looked for General Lynch, or some other general officer, to command an expedition which was ordered to effect a crossing into Canada at this point, and that arrangements were being made to a secure transportation, etc. He at the same time requested myself and the other officers present, to assist him in making the necessary arrangements, which we did.

The night of the 31st of May, being the time appointed for crossing; and as Gen. Lynch or no other general officer had arrived; and as I was the senior officer present, Capt. Hynes informed me that I should command the expedition, and proceeded verbally to give me a few general instructions, as to what I should attempt on the other side. I received no written instructions, and had no map of the country.

I at once instructed the officers to look up the men, and have them ready to march at a moment's notice; and at 11 o'clock P. M., received a written order from Captain Hynes, placing me in command of the expedition.

The number of men assembled here, which was reported to me, was about eight hundred (800)—detachments from the following regiments: 13th Infantry, Col. John O'Neill; 17th Infantry, Col. Owen Starr; 18th Infantry, Lieut. Col. Grace; 7th Infantry, Col. John Hoy; and two (2) companies from Indiana under Captain Haggerty; but the number of men that could be got together when we crossed did not exceed six hundred (600) men.

About 12 o'clock the men commenced moving to a point called Lower Black-rock, about three miles down the river; and at 3.30 A. M., on the 1st of June, all of the men, with the arms and ammunition, were on board four canal boats, and towed across the Niagara River to a point on the Canadian side, called Waterloo; and at 4 o'clock A. M., the Irish flag was planted on British soil by Col. Starr, who had command of the first two boats.

On landing I immediately ordered the telegraph wires leading from the town to be cut; and sent a party to destroy the railroad bridge leading to Port Colborne.

Col. Starr, in command of the Kentucky and Indiana troops, proceeded through the town of Erie to the Old Fort, some three miles distant (up the river) and occupied it for a short time, hoisting the Irish flag.

I then waited on the Reeve of Fort Erie, and requested him to see some of the citizens of the place and have them furnish rations for my men, at the same time assuring him that no depredations on the citizens would be permitted by me, as we had come to drive out British authority from the soil, and not for the purpose of pillaging the citizens. My request for provisions was promptly complied with.

About 10 o'clock A. M., I moved into camp on Newbiggin's Farm, situated on Frenchman's Creek, four miles down the river from Fort Erie, where I remained till 10 o'clock P. M.

During the afternoon, Capt. Donohue of the 18th, while out in command of a foraging party, on the road leading to Chippewa, came up with the enemy's scouts, who fled at his approach. Later in the afternoon, I sent Col. Hoy with one hundred (100) men on the same road. He also came up with some scouts about six miles from camp. Here I had him to halt.

By this time, 8 o'clock P. M., I had received information that a large force f the enemy—said to be five thousand strong—with artillery, were advancing in two columns—one from the direction of Chippewa, and the other from Port Colborne; also, that troops from Port Colborne were to attack me from the lake side.

Here truth compels me to make an admission that I would fain keep from the public. Many of the men who crossed over with me the night before, managed to leave the command during the day—some recrossed to Buffalo, and others remained in houses around Fort Erie.

On account of this shameful desertion, and the fact that arms had been sent with me for eight hundred (800) men, I had to destroy three hundred (300) stand of arms to prevent them falling into the hands of the enemy. At this time I could not depend on more than five hundred (500) men—about one tenth the reported number of the enemy, which I knew were surrounding me—rather a critical position; but I had been sent to accomplish a certain object, and I was determined to succeed

At 10 o'clock P. M., I broke camp and marched towards Chippewa; and at midnight changed direction and moved on the Limestone Ridge road, leading towards Ridgeway—halting a few hours on the way to rest the men: this for the purpose of meeting the column advancing from Port Colborne. My object was to get between the two columns, and, if possible, defeat one of them before the other could come to its assistance.

At about 7 o'clock A. M., 2d of June, when within three miles of Ridgeway, Col. Owen Starr, in command of the advanced guard, came up with the advance of the enemy mounted, and drove them some distance till he got within sight of their skirmish line, which extended on both sides of the road about half a mile.

By this time, we could hear the whistle of the railroad cars, which brought them from Port Colborne. I immediately advanced my skirmishers, and formed line of battle behind temporary breast-works, made of rails, on a road leading to Fort Erie, and running parallel with the enemy's line. The skirmishing was kept up over half an hour, when perceiving the enemy flanking me on both sides, and not being able to draw out his centre, which was partially protected by thick timber, I fell back a few hundred yards and formed a new line. The enemy seeing I had only a few men, (about four hundred,) and supposing that we had commenced a retreat, advanced rapidly in pursuit. When they got close enough, we gave them a volley and then charged them, driving them nearly three miles through the town of Ridgeway. In their hasty retreat, they threw away knapsacks, guns and everything that was likely to retard their speed, and left some ten or twelve killed and twenty-five or thirty wounded, with twelve prisoners in our hands. Amongst the killed was Lieut. McAhern, and amongst the wounded Lieut. Ruth, both of the Queen's Own. I gave up the pursuit about a mile beyond Ridgeway.

Although we had met and defeated the enemy, yet our position was still a very critical one. The reported strength of the enemy engaged in the fight was fourteen hundred (1400), composed of the Queen's Own, the 13th Hamilton Battalion, and other troops. A regiment which had left Port Colborne, was said to be on the road to reinforce them. I also knew that the column from Chippewa would hear of the fight, and in all probability would move up in my rear.

Thus situated, and not knowing what was going on elsewhere, I decided that my best policy was to return to Fort Erie, and ascertain if crossings had been made at other points, and if so, I was willing to sacrifice myself and my noble little command for the sake of leaving the way open, as I felt satisfied that a large proportion of the enemy's forces had been concentrated against me.

I collected a few of my own wounded and put them in wagons, and for want of transportation, had to leave six others in charge of the citizens who promised to look after them, and bury the dead of both sides. I then divided my command, and sent one half under Col. Starr down the railroad to destroy it, and burn the bridges; and with the other half took the pike road leading to Fort Erie. Col. Starr got to the old fort about the same time that we did to the village of Fort Erie (4 o'clock P. M.) He left the men there under the command of Lieut.-Col. Spaulding, and joined me in a skirmish with a company of the

Welland Battery, which had arrived there from Port Colborne in the morning, and which picked up a few of our men who had straggled from the command the day before; also a few who had basely fled on the approach of the enemy at Ridgeway. They had those men prisoners on board of the steamer Robb. The skirmish lasted about fifteen minutes. The enemy firing from the houses, three or four men were killed, and some eight or ten were wounded on each side.

It was here that Lieut.-Col. Bailey was wounded while gallantly leading the advance on one side of the town. We took some forty-five (45) of the enemy prisoners, among them Capt. King, who was wounded, (leg since amputated,) Lieut. McDonald, Royal Navy, and commander of the steamer Robb, and Lieut. Numo, Royal Artillery. I then collected my men and posted Lieut.-Col. Grace with one hundred (100) men on the outskirts of the town, guarding the road leading to Chippewa, while with the remainder of the command I proceeded to the old fort.

About 6 o'clock A. M., I sent word to Capt. Hynes and our friends at Buffalo, that the enemy could surround us before morning, with five thousand (5000) men, fully provided with artillery, and that my little command, which had by this time considerably decreased, could not hold out long; but that if a movement was going on elsewhere, I was perfectly willing to make the old fort a slaughter-pen, which I knew it would be the next day if I remained. *For I would never have surrendered.*

Many of my men had not a mouthful to eat since Friday morning; and none of them had eaten anything since the night before, and all, after marching nearly forty (40) miles and fighting two battles—though the last could only, properly, be called a skirmish—they were completely worn out with hunger and fatigue.

On receiving information that no crossing had been effected elsewhere, I sent word to have transportation furnished immediately; and about 10 o'clock P. M. Capt. Hynes came from Buffalo, and informed me that he had made arrangements for us to recross the river.

Previous to this time, some of the officers and men, realizing the danger of our position, availed themselves of small boats and stole off, leaving their comrades, as they supposed, to the tender mercies of the enemy. But the greater portion of the officers and men remained until the transportation arrived, which was about 12 o'clock on the night of June 2nd; and about 2 o'clock A. M., on the morning of the 3rd, all, except a few wounded men, were safely on board a large scow attached to a tug-boat, which hauled us into American waters. Here we were hailed by the tug Harrison, belonging to the U. S. steamer Michigan, having on board one 12-pounder pivot gun, which fired across our bows and threatened to sink us unless we hauled-to and surrendered. With the request we complied, not only because we feared the 12-pounder, or the still more powerful guns of the Michigan, which lay close by, but because we respected the authority of the United States, in defence of which many of us had fought and bled during the late war. We would have as readily surrendered to an infant bearing the authority of the United States, as to Acting Master Morris, of the tug Harrison, who is himself an Englishman. The number thus surrendered was three hundred and seventeen men, including officers.

The officers were taken on board the "Michigan," and were well treated by

Capt. Bryson and the gentlemanly officers of his ship; while the men were kept on the open scow, which was very filthy, without any accommodation whatever, and barely large enough for them to turn round. Part of the time the rain poured down on them in torrents.

I am not certain who is to blame for this cruel treatment; but whoever the guilty parties are, they should be loathed and despised by all men.

The men were kept on board the scow for four days, and then discharged on their own recognizance to appear at Canandaigua on the 19th inst. to answer to the charge of having violated the Neutrality Laws. The officers were admitted to bail.

The report generally circulated--and I might say generally believed—that I left my pickets out, and that they were captured by the enemy, is entirely false. Every man who remained with the command, excepting a few wounded, had the same chance of escaping that I had myself.

To the extraordinary exertions of Capt. Wm. J. Hynes,* Senator Fitzgerald, and our friends of Buffalo, P. O'Day, F. B. Gallagher, Hugh Mooney, James Whelan, Capt. James Doyle, John Connors, Edward Frawley, James J. Crowley, M. T. Lynch, James Cronin, and Michael Dunahey, we are indebted for being able to escape from the Canadian side. Col. H. R. Stagg and Capt. McConvery of Buffalo were also very efficient in doing everything in their power for us. Col. Stagg had started from Buffalo with about two hundred and fifty (250) men to reinforce us, but the number was too small to be of any use, and he was ordered to return. Much praise is due to Drs. Trowbridge and Blanchard of Buffalo, and Surgeon Donnelly of Pittsburgh, for their untiring attendance on the wounded.

All who were with us acted their parts so nobly that I feel a little delicacy in making special mention of any, and shall not do so except in two instances. One in the case of Michael Cochrane, color sergeant of the Indianapolis Co., whose gallantry and daring was conspicuous throughout the fight at Ridgeway. I have since learned that he was severely wounded, and is in the hands of the enemy; the other in that of Major John C. Canty, who lived at Fort Erie. He risked everything he possessed on earth, and acted his part gallantly on the field.

On account of being made a prisoner so soon, and not being able to get complete reports from the regimental commanders, this report is not as complete as I could wish it to be; and as those officers are not now subject to my orders, I would respectfully request that you order each regimental commander who was with the expedition, to forward the names of the officers and men who basely deserted the command, that they may forever be expelled from the Army of Ireland, and their names forwarded to the different circles throughout the country, so that they may be held up to the ridicule and contempt of all honest and patriotic Irishmen.

---

* Capt. Hynes, in reporting to me, verbally, the efforts he had made to procure transportation and get us back across the river, with that peculiar modesty which is all his own, took great credit to himself for his skillful management of the affair. But subsequent reports of F. B. Gallagher, P. O'Day, and numerous other citizens of Buffalo, go to show, that if they had not taken the matter entirely out of his hands, and attended to it themselves in spite of him, through his presumption and arrogance we should likely have had to remain on the other side until the enemy came up the following morning.

In the fight at Ridgeway and the skirmish at Fort Erie, as near as I can ascertain, our loss was eight killed and fifteen wounded. Among the killed was Lieut. E. R. Lonnergan, a brave young officer of Buffalo. Of the enemy, thirty (30) were killed, and one hundred (100) wounded.

I refer you to the accompanying reports of Col. Owen Starr, Col. John Hoy, Capts. Shields, Conlon, and Munday, for individual acts of bravery; and would recommend that all officers who remained with the command, receive promotion to one grade higher than they had, and the sergeants, corporals, and privates recommended by their immediate commanding officers, receive promotion to fill their places. I would also recommend that Capt. Rodolph Fitzpatrick, of my staff, be appointed Major in the A. G. Dept.

(Signed) JOHN O'NEILL,

Brig. Genl. I. R. A.

NOTE.—The number of the enemy killed and wounded, was made up from personal observation, reports of prisoners, and general report at the time. I believe, however, that the figures are too high, but I have not been able to get the exact numbers.

APPENDIX.

REPORT OF MAJOR DANIEL MURPHY.

BRIDGEPORT, Ct., June, 1870.

GEN. JOHN O'NEILL,

Dear Sir, and Brother:—In compliance with your request for a report of my connection with the late disastrous movement on Canada, and of the part I took in that affair, I hereby most respectfully state the following facts:

On May 16th, 1870, I received orders from the Headquarters of the F. B., (of which I have not a copy,) directing me (as captain) to prepare my company at once for a forward movement, as final orders would be issued in a few days.

I need hardly assure you that I was much surprised at this, for it will be remembered by many of the delegates of the New York Congress, (held April 19th, 1870,) as well as by yourself, I presume, that I declined having anything to do with a movement which I believed to be premature, and supported only by a fragment of the Irish people. This sentiment I gave utterance to in the Congress; and I may here add, it was the sentiment of the best men composing that body outside Manhattan, and Gen. J. J. Donnelly. I went further, by informing that body that they could not depend on any men from Connecticut to inaugurate the movement, as I believed the Organization in that State to be demoralized, which assertion afterwards proved true. At these remarks Gen. J. J. Donnelly honored me by descending from his dignified position, as Speaker of the House, in order to reply and counteract their apparent effects, if possible. This he accomplished to his entire satisfaction, being well adapted and fully competent to control the opinions of such an audience as he was then addressing, to neither of which qualities do I lay claim. This gentleman concluded his speech with the following declaration, as near as I can remember, and for the falsity of which I hope he will now answer to the Irish people, or at least to that portion of them who contributed of their limited means, as far as in them lay, to the support of the F. B., and the purchase of that war material which was squandered on the frontier and stolen by the Canadians:

"It makes little difference whether Capt. Murphy or the men of Bridgeport take part in the movement or not; whether the men of Connecticut take part in it or not; there are men enough without them, who have had their transportation money in their pockets and their rations cooked for the past week, and the movement will be made." Here I dropped the matter with the remark that, if they were determined to move, I should place no barrier in the way, and subsequent events prove that I have kept my promise. Did Gen. Donnelly keep his? In order to show the value of promises made at those Congresses, I will cite a few instances, and most respectfully ask those who ought to know, were the promises redeemed? W. J. Davis, of Brooklyn, promised $5,000.00 in seven days; Gen. Donnelly the same; others promised according to the temperature of their pseudo patriotism, the whole amounting (on paper) to $15,000.00. According to the report of the military committee $30,000.00 was deemed necessary to a successful inauguration of the movement, but by some mathematical calculations this sum was subsequently reduced to $15,000.00, which was to be paid into Headquarters in seven days after the adjournment of Congress. I am now informed by you, General, and Gen. Donnelly, also, that only about $2,000.00 of this amount was received at Headquarters in thirty days, of which the few patriotic Irish Nationalists I represented, (after promising nothing,) furnished $250.00.

Now, then, in the face of these facts and figures, on whose shoulders will history lay the cause of that disastrous movement, with scarce one dollar in the treasury? I will leave that question for you, General, and General Donnelly, also, to answer. If desired, I will give the names of all the parties promising money at the New York Congress, that the world may know who those parties are who urged us on to the cannon's mouth and then deserted us. To go back to the preliminary order already alluded to, upon the receipt of it, I immediately concluded to be there myself at least. I informed a few friends of what was on foot, and, also, of my decision in the matter; the result of this was that on Saturday, May 21st, when final orders were received, about 30 names were on the roll, all of whom were ready and anxious to be the first in the field. What were we to do on Monday morning when these men expected to leave for the front? Not one dollar was in the treasury, (in fact, we had neither treasury nor organization,) but, by the extraordinary exertion of a few devoted sons of Ireland, the requisite amount (three hundred dollars) was raised, and at 11.30 P. M., we were all on board the train for St. Albans via Springfield, some of us paying our own fare.

I might mention here, that before leaving Bridgeport, Capt. Fitzpatrick was elected captain of the company, I having previously received an appointment as Major, which position it was not my intention to hold when in the field. On arriving in Springfield on Tuesday morning, April 24th, we found a company from Portland, Connecticut, under the command of a Capt. Ahern. This was the first time on the route that we learned that any one knew of the movement. We rested a few hours on the soft side of a plank board in one of the Springfield halls, kindly given to us gratis by the proprietor. At 8 o'clock A. M., we were all on board the train for St. Albans, after travelling about one hundred miles without meeting any one who knew anything of the movement, or who was bent on the same mission. I began to doubt whether there really was a movement going on or not. On arriving at White River Junction, we were reinforced by eight men from Norwich, Connecticut, and with the exception of about half a dozen more who joined us on the road, all the men on board that train bound for Canada on a hostile mission were Connecticut men. On arriving at Essex Junction, we were met by about 170 men from New York, under the command of Lieut. Col. Leddy. Somewhat encouraged at this acquisition to our numbers, and informed by some of those braggarts from New York (of whom I shall presently speak) that thousands more were coming on the next train, we sent the following dispatch to Bridgeport:

ESSEX JUNCTION, VT., May 24th, 1870.

JOHN CULLINAN :

SIR : Great excitement here ; thousands of men on the road ; send men quick.

D. MURPHY.

The result of the above was, that on the 26th, two days afterwards, 28 more men arrived at St. Albans from Bridgeport, under the command of Lieut. Francis Connery.

On arriving at St. Albans, where we expected to learn that at least the men of Boston who, five weeks previously, according to Gen. Donnelly's statement, had their transportation money in their pocket and their rations cooked, were there before us, to our great surprise they were not arrived, nor scarcely any one else, according to information received from citizens of Vermont. Intoxicated, I suppose, with an intense desire to meet the enemy of our race and country in the open field, we did not believe the citizens of Vermont. Gen. Donnelly here informed me that Gen. Lewis had crossed the border with about 200 men, and that two or three hundred more were on the way to reinforce him, and that Gen. O'Neill was at the front and would make a crossing next morning at three o'clock with all the available force he could command ; that I was expected to take command of the Connecticut men (which now numbered about 70) and make a forced march to the front in order to be there in time for the crossing. It was now about 7 o'clock P. M. as we took up our line of march for the front by the Fairfield and Highgate road, 14 miles from Franklin, the New York men taking the Sheldon road, 19 miles from Franklin. There being no provision made for hard tack, we halted about two miles outside the town, sent back for three days' rations, paid for it with money subscribed by the citizens of Bridgeport, and at 10 o'clock P. M. started for the front under the direction of a guide, who, I might here remark, guided us seven miles out of the way and over the roughest road it has ever been my experience to travel, and in one of the darkest nights. Now it may be said that the men of Bridgeport commenced to prove themselves Irishmen worthy of the name ; during that long and tedious march over the rugged road of Northern Vermont, they never faltered, they never murmured. They knew their instructions, and, as thorough revolutionists, they appreciated the value of time by moving forward swiftly and pushing the Portland men, who, I must say, showed a very poor disposition to get to the front. As for the men of Norwich, they could not be managed ; they put up in a barn by the road-side. In consequence of the seven miles extra inflicted on us by our faithful English guide, for such we found him to be when too late, we did not arrive at the front until 5 o'clock in the morning of the 25th ; every Bridgeport man was at his post with a single exception, and this through mistake, by mixing up with the New York men before leaving St. Albans.

By this it will be seen that in the space of about thirty hours we traversed 350 miles of railroad, and marched through thirty miles of mud. On arriving at the front almost exhausted, what a scene presented itself to men who had already been informed that there were men enough without them ; here and there were seated a few squads of men ; some were lying around loose in a demoralized condition ; and, God knows, I could not blame them, for, perhaps some of them were told the same story that was told to me ; perhaps many of them received the same insult that I received ; but, whether they did or not, in my humble opinion they were in no condition for an offensive movement. The first cheering news we received was that Gen. O'Neill had not men enough to cross the line, that the brave Gen. Lewis had deserted his post, and that the whole affair had gone up. We hoped against hope that we were not deceived by some one ; but in vain—we were ; and we hope now, and trust, that no matter what the difficulty between the authors of that unfortunate movement, and other contending factions, might be, a satisfactory explanation will be given to the parties who risked their lives in such a hopeless affair, and also to an outraged people who supported the movement and furnished the transportation and war material. About 8 o'clock I received warning to prepare for marching orders at a moment's notice. For some time it was a question in my mind whether I should obey this order or not. I really had no command, there were only about 60 men from Connecticut, half of whom would not go into the enemy's country without five hundred men went, and did not go. It was now about 10 o'clock, and the braggarts from New York, who left St. Albans the same time we did, had not yet arrived. I finally concluded as the least of two evils to go to the front ; so did Capt. Fitzpatrick of the Bridgeport company, whose name deserves special mention here for bravery and gallant conduct in the presence of the enemy—also the company he had the honor of commanding. Capt. Ahern and his lieutenant, of the Portland company, after failing to induce their men to meet the enemy, shouldered muskets themselves and fell into the ranks with the men of Bridgeport, at half past 10 o'clock. Capt. Fitzpatrick's company, now numbering about 40 men, were inspected by Gen. Donnelly, and I may say here, they were the only men on the ground who were subjected to inspection. About half past 11 we were ordered to march, and in less than half an hour we were engaged with the enemy. Before leaving the road leading from the United States to Canada, Francis Caraher, of Bridgeport, fell seriously wounded, while crossing an open lot which led to the woods back of Richards's house. Lieut. Hope, also of Bridgeport, fell seriously wounded and was carried from the field under a shower of British bullets by Sergeant T. J. O'Donnell, of the same company. On arriving on the summit of a hill in the woods, a brisk fire was kept up with the enemy, the colors of the Burlington men being placed there by Capt. Fitzpatrick, around which every man from Bridgeport, with a few others, rallied. At this time about 70 men were present ; where the remainder of them went, I cannot inform you ; but I think some of them went to the rear. Soon after, I was ordered by you, General, to take charge of the men while you went back to hurry up the New York men, who left St. Albans when we did, and had not yet arrived, it being now 2 o'clock. Before assuming command, we retreated out of range of the enemy's guns, where we remained until J. Boyle O'Reilly returned with the news of your arrest, whereupon I despatched a corporal's guard (not having but about two good ones) to ascertain whether Gen. Donnelly and his corporal's guard were still shut up in Richards's house and barn. In an hour they returned with the information that he and his men had escaped. At this time (4 o'clock) we had about 40 men, and, judging it useless to remain there longer, I returned with my command to the camp ; here we met the New York men for the first time since we parted from them at St. Albans. They managed to get to the front about ten hours later than we did; and here, amidst a set of far more demoralized men than it had been our misfortune to meet in the same place in 1866, we came to the conclusion that we, at least, were humbugged badly, that the representations made to us were false, utterly so; and then steered our course homeward, after caring for our wounded men and providing for their transit to St. Albans, and then to Bridgeport. On our arrival in the first-named place, we met at least 150 men from various parts of Connecticut, and a fine body of men they were; I believe I can safely say they were much the finest and best conducted body of men we saw at St. Albans. On the 27th of May we were arrested and sent to jail.

In conclusion, I have only a few words to say, and they are to those who might be drawn into a similar movement hereafter by any man or faction of men. Never go to Canada on a hostile mission, for, just as sure as you do, you will fail, if Uncle Sam is not at your back. Never join an organization of Irish Nationalists (so called) if they are not united; you are only helping to prolong the quarrel and indefinitely postpone the freedom of Ireland. You cannot expect that a set of men, who are always quarrelling with each other for power and favor, when the enemies of our unfortunate country are blazing away at our fathers and mothers with the fatal quiver of starvation, will be men enough to forget those quarrels when the enemy is vanquished. No; they will carry this feeling with them to the verge of the grave, and perhaps further. We have no quarrel with any of those factions; and feeling that we have done our duty, we now withdraw from any further connection with any faction calling itself by any name. We have attended a few congresses of the Organization, and heard nothing but lying and scoundrelism, the most solemn pledges broken, and all the gasconade when outside the congress hall vanish into thin air. It is very convenient in case of failure to have one man upon whose shoulders the odium of such failures may forever rest, but in my opinion (and I know from experience what I am talking about) the cause of the failures is justly attributed to the gas-blowers who attended those congresses, and there made promises which they never made an effort to redeem. This is why I think the names of those men should be known. I now close this story of my experience with Fenianism, and with it close my connection with any of its present contending factions.

Wishing you success in anything you may undertake, I remain, dear General, very truly your friend,

D. MURPHY, Ex-Major I. R. A.

EXTRACTS FROM GEN. DONNELLY'S REPORT.

* * * * * * * *

On my arrival in Boston, I found that but one circle in the State could be said to be actually in existence—the O'Neill circle of Cambridge. The time was too short for reorganization of circles, and at a meeting of the prominent men amongst those who had been members of the Organization, it was decided to ignore the circles and to appoint in their stead transportation committees for the various localities, the chairmen of which would form a central committee, which would meet in Boston at the call of its chairman. This plan was found to work admirably. It gave everybody an opportunity to work, and all who could be reached did go to work with a will. I visited Providence, and set the ball in motion at that point and vicinity in a similar manner. Nothing could exceed the enthusiasm of the people at this time. All former dissensions seemed to be forgotten, and all Irish Organizations vied with each other in the work of procuring men and means. The result was that on the 18th day of April a force of one thousand men could have been marched from the districts above named. The enemy, however, had in the meantime possessed himself of very correct information of our intentions, and prepared for our reception to an extent that induced a change in the time of making the attempt to cross the border.

* * * * * * *

On my return to Boston, May 8th, I found the enthusiasm of the people very much cooled off by my delay in New York, which *you* know was unavoidable; but in Providence, Lawrence, Lowell, and many other places, the committees were working very energetically. After repeated meetings, the people of Boston were again at work in earnest; new companies were formed, and enlistments were proceeding rapidly; companies from the I. R. B. and other Organizations tendered their services; the officers of the Savage circles called upon me and tendered their support. The President of the convention of Irish Societies called a meeting of that body, the members of which pledged their support. Many civic societies called meetings, voted a portion of their funds, and appointed committees to aid in raising transportation for men to the front. Altogether the situation was very encouraging, and I left Boston for Vermont on the 17th of April with the firmest conviction that Massachusetts and Rhode Island would furnish at least one thousand men for the first movement. Before leaving, I issued the final orders to move the troops so as to have them arrive at St. Albans at 6 o'clock A. M. on the 24th of April, and, to the utmost of my ability, impressed upon the central committee the necessity of prompt action and no delays. For this I made out and gave them the time of the trains starting from the various points, so as to unite at White River Junction, Vermont. My desire was to remain and bring the troops forward with me; but, for reasons well known to you, my presence in Vermont was deemed necessary for at least a week before the move.

* * * * * * * *

The hour (5 o'clock P. M., May 23d) had now arrived for the men to start from Boston, and if anything was wanting to convince me that they would come on time, it was furnished in a dispatch from Boston to the superintendent of the Vermont Central Railroad, asking him to send cars enough to White River Junction to transport one thousand men. I watched the depot until I saw the cars sent, and then returned to the house of a friend.

* * * * * * * *

I consider the conduct of the officers at the rear as anything but soldierly. After your arrest, their first duty was to ascertain who the ranking officer was, and report to him for duty, instead of lying around the camp or holding town meetings in the fields; and if, as I am informed, they believed me and my handful of men to be shut up with the prospect of capture, their failure to come forward and relieve me was cowardly in the extreme. I would have gone farther to relieve any one of them.

After all, it is better as it was. The whole movement failed on Tuesday morning, with the failure of the men from Boston to arrive on the 6 o'clock train, as agreed upon. After that time, nothing could be done to make the movement a success. We might have made a pretty good fight, if we could have got 500 or 600 men across at Pigeon Hill. If the New York men had been up in time, you no doubt would have captured Eccles Hill; but we would have been flanked out of it in our turn, for the enemy had 1500 men there by 3 o'clock P. M., and with the New York men we would only have had about 300 men by that hour—a force totally inadequate to hold the position, as, when turned, it had no advantages. If, on the other hand, all or one half of the men we were promised, had arrived on time, I think there is no doubt but that we could have been successful. Nothing but the failure of the men to arrive at the proper time prevented the carrying out of your plans successfully. The enemy was totally unprepared to receive us on Tuesday morning. Had 400 men arrived in St. Albans at 6 o'clock in the morning, I could have taken them into St. Johns by railroad without the slightest opposition. There was not a soldier in St. Johns until about 4 o'clock P. M. I could have been there at 9 o'clock A. M. Had I succeeded in occupying St. Johns, I would have been in a position to threaten Montreal, supported by you with what force could be spared from the camp at Pigeon Hill. I would therefore have occupied the attention of all the forces the enemy could have mustered for at least four days, which would have given you all the opportunity you desired to place our war material on the Canadian border, in the hands of men who would then have had the courage to use it.

Gen. Starr's command would have met with no opposition until he reached the vicinity of St. Johns, as the enemy could not turn upon him without exposing his flank and rear to an attack of our combined forces at St. Johns and Pigeon Hill, besides uncovering Montreal, only 20 miles from St. Johns.

It may be said that Montreal had but little to fear from a force of 400 men, even if I had occupied St. Johns. But it must be borne in mind, that had one half the number of men arrived on time, which we were most positively assured would come, my force would have been increased to 1500 men on Wednesday night—exclusive of Lewis's men or Sinnott's expedition—a force amply sufficient to hold in check any force the enemy could muster south of the St. Lawrence at that time. Even as late as Friday they had but 2000 men. It must also be remembered that all communications would have been cut south of the river, which would have prevented the mustering of the militia in that district in a great measure. The simple fact of the capture of St. Johns would have made it necessary for a large force to remain in Montreal and Quebec to take care of the Fenians at these points, who would certainly have shown their hand had we been at all successful in our first efforts. The occupation of the points designated in your plan was, on Tuesday morning, a very easy feat to accomplish. But on Wednesday, at noon, it was impossible, even with a considerable force, as the enemy was then occupying these points, and could have held them against such troops as we could have brought against them. Neither theirs nor ours were the kind of troops to attack a position with, as neither were sufficiently drilled or organized, and the force occupying the position in such a contest was the one likely to be victorious. Hence the necessity of moving before the enemy was prepared. That we calculated correctly in this respect is well known and admitted, as it is known to every one who was near the line at that time, that the volunteers did not receive orders to march until Tuesday morning, notwithstanding the fact that the government was notified at 4 o'clock Monday afternoon, that the Fenians were on the move. After the officers received their orders, they were obliged to collect their men, in many cases scattered over a whole township, attending to their farms or their workshops; a work that required days rather than hours to accomplish. Never was a more complete surprise effected, and nothing but the tardiness of the men in coming forward at the time agreed upon prevented the occupation of the whole country south of the St. Lawrence within three days, and without the loss of as many men as were sacrificed in our failure to obtain even a foothold.

But why were our men so much behind time? We believed, not without the most positive assurance, that Vermont would furnish at least 700 men at Franklin by daylight Tuesday morning; that Massachusetts and Rhode Island would send 1000 men to St. Albans by six o'clock A. M.; that 200 picked men would be at Island Pond about the same time; that New York and Brooklyn would furnish 600 men on Tuesday evening at 6 o'clock; that from western New York, Albany, Troy, Newark, Bridgeport and New Haven, 1500 men would arrive at Malone during Tuesday and the forenoon of Wednesday; and from each of these points we expected at least an equal number of men would arrive within forty-eight hours after the first detachments. The failure of Vermont I can account for, because I was there and could see for myself. The officer in charge of military affairs had no men. He had done nothing to organize troops. This is the man who pledged 700 men last April.

Why New York and Brooklyn sent 170 instead of 600 I have not yet learned; neither can I inform you of the reason why western New York did not furnish the 1000 men said to be ready to march across the line last April. Bridgeport furnished more men than was expected, and they arrived before they were expected. Major Murphy and Capt. Fitzpatrick did their duty certainly. Capt. Kenally of Marlboro also brought the number of men he promised. The other places mentioned were not depended upon, except Massachusetts and Rhode Island. These States, together with Vermont, were depended upon above all others, as from these States we expected men first; yet of all others, these States failed most completely, and of all the failures this to me is the most incomprehensible. I have written to get some light upon the subject, but have not yet been informed. I have inquired of the few who did come, but I am not willing to believe some of the statements my inquiries elicited. I cannot believe that the men who shook my hand on my departure from Boston, wishing me God speed, and pledging me to do all in their power to get the men ready and forward them promptly on time, would deliberately go to their homes and shrewdly wait until the fight had actually commenced before they would send the men upon whom we were depending to begin the fight. I cannot believe that, in the face of my most positive assurance that men would cross the lines on Monday night, depending upon their support on Tuesday morning, they would cold bloodedly determine to wait to learn the fate of these before they sent a man to assist them. And yet, Col. McGinniss, the officer selected by these men to command the troops from Massachusetts, instead of moving his command on Monday at 5 o'clock P. M., as he was ordered, waited until Tuesday night, and then came to St. Albans alone, and there stated, in the presence of at least fifty persons, that he was sent to ascertain whether a fight was really going on. If he was satisfied, he said, that we were fighting, he would telegraph to Massachusetts, where 3000 men were all ready to start for the front. Now, why was not a part of these men sent when it was promised they would come? Perhaps prudential considerations had something to do with the delay. If this was the case, the men of Boston may in the future have the consoling reflection that their prudence more than any and all things else contributed to the failure.

But, whatever was the cause, the men did not come, and we have therefore added another to the many failures which Irishmen have made in their struggle with the foe of their race. You and many other good men are in prison; I soon expect to keep you company, and so ends the invasion (?) of Canada. But it will be a long time before we hear the last of it. Of course you are to blame for it all. Well, that is but fair. You would have received the largest share of the praise if we had succeeded.

I notice the generalship of Pigeon Hill and Trout River is severely criticised. Well, I for one am perfectly willing that those who criticise should take the same number of men under similar circumstances and try their hand at generalship. But you ought to have had more men there, they will say. I know we ought; but how could we, when those who pledged themselves to do so, failed to send them? Some will say—indeed many have already said, "Why did you attempt to cross with so few men?" These same men would have been the first to cry out "cowards," if we had refused to cross with half that number.

I notice the press and people are severe on you, and claim you made arrangements for your arrest. I would pay no attention to this. Time will show the injustice of the foul slanders that are finding circulation among the people. Unfortunately for you, the first intelligence was carried to the rear by those who were never at the front, or were the first to run away. Among the few brave fellows who remained with me to the last, not one is found to blame you, and none had more reason to complain of your arrest than they, as its immediate effect was to shut us up in a position which was anything but agreeable.

These men were not the sort who would lightly overlook an act of cowardice in their officers.

You are to blame, however, and so am I and many others, for believing so implicitly in the promises of the people to support a movement against the enemy, when they were convinced that we were about to commence it. We ought to have known that those who make an excuse to shirk their part of the necessary preparation, would find some excuse to avoid their share of the work when it was actually begun. There is any amount of honest (?) indignation manifested at "the disgrace it has brought upon us," by those who failed in toto to perform one act or lift a finger to make it a success. But these people will prate about what wonders they were accomplishing in the way of raising men and means, when they heard of the arrest of O'Neill. But in this case, as in every other, they began too late. If they had begun their efforts to assist us sooner, you would not have been arrested. You must not understand from this that I do not believe the Irish people would support a fight, and fight as desperately for the success of their own cause as they did for the stranger, if they could be convinced that fighting was intended ; but it needs too much to convince them,—nothing less than the actual commencement of hostilities. Any one who can afford to commence hostilities against Great Britain in the name of the Irish people at his own expense, has a splendid opening for business in that line, and will undoubtedly have the support of the Irish people after he has got fairly under way.

I cannot close this without expressing my gratitude to the people of St. Albans and Burlington for their kind treatment of me whilst amongst them.

Gen. Foster, U. S. Marshal, and his deputy, J. M. Smalley, Esq., were untiring in their efforts to make my situation as comfortable as circumstances would admit, nor were their efforts confined to me alone. Both of these gentlemen used their own funds freely in feeding the men at St. Albans, and forwarding them to their homes. Mr. Brainard, who became my bail, has placed me under lasting obligations, my counsel, Guy C. Noble, Esq., noble by nature as well as by name, has my everlasting gratitude.

Very respectfully,

Your obt. servant,

J. J. DONNELLY.

SUPPLEMENT TO GENERAL REPORT.

NEW YORK, *November 1st*, 1870.

General Donnelly, whose sincerity, patriotism and courage cannot be doubted, gave up a lucrative business in Utica, N. Y., to go to Massachusetts and Rhode Island for the purpose of organizing a force in those two States to assist in commencing a movement. He repeatedly assured me that I could depend on from ten to twelve hundred men the first day, and on an equal number the second day. I have no doubt but that this promise would have been made good, if the movement had taken place before the 19th of April, as at first intended, and the General had been in Boston to personally superintend the forwarding of troops. Delay seems to have had a disastrous effect. It is not easy, however, to understand why the parties who were left in charge, and who, it appears, solemnly pledged themselves to forward the men, so utterly failed to keep their word. I have been informed that some of the wealthiest and most respectable of our countrymen in Massachusetts and Rhode Island were members of the various committees. I now ask Gen. Donnelly to furnish me with a list of their names, to be published with his report, so that the public may know the parties who could so trifle with the sacred cause of Ireland and the lives of their fellow countrymen. On Massachusetts and Rhode Island, more than on any other States, did I rely for men to commence the movement, and in none others was I so grievously disappointed. The failure of the men to arrive in time gave the enemy ample opportunity to put himself in readiness. After my arrest there was very little chance of effecting anything at any point. A great deal has been said about a lack of competent officers. Had the men been prompt in coming up, there would have been no lack of able officers, for they would have been ordered up: as it was, there was no occasion for a display of generalship.

I shall soon publish the Report of Gen. Donnelly, which reached me too late to be inserted here in full: also, the reports of the other officers who were present at Franklin, and of those at Malone and Island Pond; and of such as were to operate against the Red River expedition.

The road which Major Murphy took from St. Albans to Franklin was much shorter than that over which Col. Leddy and his men had to travel, the latter having been ordered to take said road for the purpose of arming his men at a house on the way, where some of our arms, etc., were stored. It was feared that the teams engaged to haul them to the front would not be able to get them all up before the United States soldiers, who were said to be on the way, would intercept them. The extra distance which Major Murphy and his men had to travel, through mistake of the guide, more than made up for this difference. I have not yet had a report from Col. Leddy, consequently I cannot say what excuse he has to offer for the delay in getting to camp, but all other reports which I have received go to show that his men made no great effort to get up in time.

I know that the road was bad and the men unaccustomed to marching, and no doubt hungry. Yet, of all the men whom I expected on the border, I depended more upon those from New York to overcome such difficulties particularly when they were told that I had crossed the line, and expected them to hurry to my assistance. There were plenty of provisions for them in camp.

SENDING THE MEN HOME.

In behalf of the Fenian Brotherhood and the cause of Irish liberty, I beg to return my sincere thanks to the Hon. Wm. M. Tweed, of New York, who has forever endeared himself to the gratitude of the Irish people, by his great kindness and liberality in furnishing transportation to their homes for a large number of the men who went to the border.

IN PRISON.

Soon after my arrest, several gentlemen in and around Burlington, Vt., came to me and offered to go on my bonds. The commissioner who first fixed the bail, having placed it at twenty thousand dollars, considerable time was lost in having it reduced to fifteen thousand. In the meantime, one of our officers, Col. Hugh McGinnis, who had been bailed out at St. Albans, having promised to furnish indemnity bonds on his return home, failed to report. (It would appear that he went to Chicago, where he was taken sick, and subsequently died.) This, together with some underhand work, discouraged the parties who had offered to go on my bonds, caused them to hesitate and delay, and finally back out altogether. The delay thus caused prevented me from writing to parties who would have bailed me out at first. The following named gentlemen, when they heard how the matter stood, kindly volunteered to furnish the bail: Rev. H. Quigley, D.D., pastor of Erin, Wisconsin; Daniel F. Keefe, Glens Falls, N. Y.; George Francis Train, James Lackey, Washington, D. C.; D. F. McCarthy, Faribault, Minn.; Col. Wm. F. Atkinson and Brother, Port Huron, Mich. But as these parties were not residents of Burlington, or personally known to the judge who had charge of the case, they could only give a bond of indemnity to some party or parties who were residents. This again caused considerable delay, and before the matter could be finally arranged, the time for my trial was at hand. I remained in Burlington jail two months, during which time I received much kindness at the hands of the efficient and gentlemanly sheriff, L. M. Drew, and his amiable lady; also, from the citizens of Burlington generally: Mr. John Dullahan, J. B. Scully, P. H. Kennedy, Major J. J. Monaghan, Capts. Carlton, Cronin, Murphy and a host of others were untiring in their exertions to render my prison life as comfortable as possible, and cause me to forget the almost entire neglect of my Fenian friends outside of Burlington. At the time I felt very much hurt over this neglect, but when I take into consideration the efforts that had been put forth to vilify and misrepresent me, I can readily find an excuse for it. A man who had been represented to our people as a "coward" and a "traitor to Ireland," could hardly expect any better treatment. Against these charges I have no defence to make. If there is a single Irishman in the Fenian Brotherhood or out of it, who really believes me to be either a "coward" or a "traitor to Ireland," I can afford to pity him.

After my trial, I remained two months and a half in Windsor prison, Vermont, where the kind hearted and gentlemanly superintendent, J. A. Pollard, and his estimable family, together with the chaplain of the prison, Franklin Butler, the warden, S. T. Lull, and the gentlemen composing the prison guard, did all that they could to make myself and Col. J. H. Brown, who was in prison with me, happy and contented. Here again the citizens were very kind to us.

I desire to return my heartfelt thanks to the kind and generous friends, Patrick Carty, Essex Junction; Jerry H. Flinn, Milton; John Dullahan, J. B. Scully, P. H. Kennedy, Captains Cronin, Murphy and others of Burlington, Vermont; who, on learning of the destitute circumstances of my family, sent for them, and made provision for their support during my imprisonment; and also to the following gentlemen for their kind donations towards the same object:

Hon. Wm. M. Evarts, late Attorney General, United States, Windsor, Vt.	$50 00
Hon. E. H. Stoughton, Windsor, Vt.	50 00
Major-General B. F. Butler, Lowell, Mass.	20 00
John Dullahan, from self and others, Burlington, Vt.	24 00
Dr. E. Donnelly, from himself and others, Pittsburgh, Pa.	20 00
Thomas Keefe, John O'Neil, and others, employees of the Vermont Central Railroad	63 50
Allen, Larkin & O'Brien circle, F. B., Fort Laramie, Wyoming Territory, per Sergeants John Glynn and P. O'Keefe	26 00
James Lackey, Washington, D. C.	5 00
Thomas J. Barton, Waltham, Mass.	10 00
P. Donohue, Boston, Mass	25 00
Unknown friend, through Marshal Foster	25 00

Mr. Phelps, attorney, at Burlington, Vt., will please accept my thanks for his kindness and services, rendered legally and otherwise; also, the Messrs. Smalley.

MY RELEASE.

Although sentenced to two years' imprisonment, I did not expect to remain in confinement that length of time. Neither did I at first look for so early a release, until I heard of the numerous petitions gotten up in almost every section of the country, signed by all classes of citizens. The first of which I had any knowledge was started in St. Louis, and presented to the President in person, on the occasion of his visit to that city, by Mayor Cole, Judge Daily, Hon. Erastus Wells and others. Afterwards, when such men as Generals B. F. Butler and N. P. Banks of Massachusetts, Gen. Schenck of Ohio, Hon. James M. Cavanagh of Montana, Hon. Horace Greeley and Hon. Thomas Murphy of New York, and hundreds of the first men of the country, as well as numerous Organizations, interested themselves in the matter, I knew that, as these parties represented the wish of the American people, the Chief Executive of the nation would feel justified in granting our release, and on receipt of the following letter was satisfied that we had not much longer to remain in prison :

NEW YORK, OCTOBER 4, 1870.

GEN. JOHN O'NEILL :

DEAR SIR : Although I have not the pleasure of a personal acquaintance with you, I sympathized with you in your misfortune and imprisonment. I thought that the time had come for your liberation, and that I would do something towards it. A week ago I spoke to Mr. Greeley about you and fellow prisoners. He told me he would use all his influence for you ; but as he was going to the West the next day, he had not time until his return. But Mr. Greeley told me to go to Thomas Murphy, Collector of the Port of New York, and say to him that Mr. Greeley wanted him to act in your behalf immediately. I did so. Mr. Murphy took hold of the matter earnestly ; saw President Grant about the matter last Friday, who said, that immediately on his return to Washington, he would issue a proclamation for your release. You may expect it every moment ; but keep this private until you receive it. Many others interested themselves in the matter ; Gen. Woodford, Gen. Porter, and your friends of the "Irish Republican Central Club of New York." After your liberation, I would like to meet you some afternoon, at 3 o'clock, at Sweeny's Hotel, New York.

Your friend,

THOMAS MCGRANE, 247 E. 30th St., New York.

When the President got to Washington, the indictments on which we were tried were written for, and, as soon as they arrived, and the necessary papers could be made out, our pardons were granted. I now beg to return my sincere thanks, on behalf of myself and fellow prisoners, to the numerous parties who interested themselves in procuring our release.

JOHN O'NEILL.

SPEECH OF GENERAL JOHN O'NEILL,

At his Trial at Windsor, July 30, 1870.

MAY it please your Honors, I feel that I occupy a very awkward position as a man who loves and reveres the laws of the land—as a man who has fought and bled to preserve those laws—I cannot but feel the awkwardness of my position in standing before this Court charged with the crime of violating those laws. As a soldier of the American Republic, I served, as the record will show, honestly and faithfully. Before the breaking out of the late unfortunate war, I was a soldier in the regular army. I enlisted in 1857, and successively served as a private, as a corporal, as a sergeant, as a sergeant-major, brevet second lieutenant, first lieutenant, and captain; and resigned after having been recommended for the position of Colonel on account of services rendered by me in the cause of my country, and in defence of her laws. I did not feel justified in remaining in the army, because I had been disqualified for active service in the field, having been severely wounded during the siege of Knoxville, in the latter part of 1863.

With your kind permission I will read one or two short letters received from gentlemen distinguished in the army. I have a number of such letters, but have only two or three with me. The first is from Major-General Stoneman, dated Headquarters 23d Army Corps, March 8th, 1864:

I knew Lieut. O'Neill well on the Peninsula, and as a brave and worthy officer, in whose judgment and capacity I had the greatest confidence. I hope he will receive the promotion to which his merits entitle him, that of a field officer in a colored regiment.

GEORGE STONEMAN, Maj. Gen. Commanding Corps.

I beg leave to remark that after being wounded I was placed on a military examining board at Nashville, Tenn. While there I felt that I would like to have command of a colored cavalry regiment, and made application for such a command, hence the letter of Gen. Stoneman.

The next is from Gen. Judah, dated Headquarters 2d Division, 23d Army Corps, in camp near Mossy Creek, Tenn., March 7th, 1864:

It gives me pleasure to state that, from personal observation, I deem Lieut. John O'Neill, of the 5th Indiana Cavalry, one of the most gallant and efficient officers it has been my duty to command. His daring and services have been conspicuous, and I trust he may receive what he has so ably merited—his promotion.

H. M. JUDAH, Brig. Gen. Com. Div.

The following indorsement appears on a resignation which I tendered whilst first Lieutenant of the Indiana Cavalry. This resignation I tendered because I felt that I had been unjustly dealt with by the colonel of my regiment. The commanding general seems to have held the same opinion, as will appear from the following endorsement on my resignation :

HEADQUARTERS, CAVALRY CORPS, PARIS, KY., April 7, 1864.

Disapproved and respectfully forwarded. This is an excellent officer, too valuable indeed to be lost to the service. He was severely wounded at Taswell, Tennessee, under Col. Graham, last December, and is estimated as one of the best officers of my command. This is not the only resignation which has been offered on account of promotions of inferiors having been made in the 5th Indiana Cavalry over the heads of superiors, based upon political or other considerations, and altogether regardless of merit. By this system, junior and meritorious officers find themselves cut off from all hope of advancement, and compelled to serve subordinate to others for whose qualifications they can entertain no respect. While therefore I disapprove his resignation for the public good, I would respectfully urge that some policy be initiated or recommended by which officers can see the way open for their advancement according to merit.

S. D. STURGES, Brig. Gen. Com'g. Corps.

These, with other communications, of a similar character, prove conclusively that although I have, as acknowledged yesterday, violated the laws of the land, I still love those laws. I revere them, and when the opportunity came, and the occasion required, I showed my willingness to fight, and, if necessary, to die for them.

As one of a persecuted race—as one who had suffered at the hands of tyranny and oppression in my native land, I came to this country full of hopeful confidence that I should enjoy that liberty which was denied me at home. I came to America like thousands of my countrymen, because I had been oppressed in my native land. I came to this country for the purpose of making a dutiful citizen of the land of my adoption, and except in this instance, and perhaps another of a similar character, I think my past history and record will show that I have made a good citizen, and that I have been willing when called upon to offer up my life for the land of my adoption. But while I have felt the duties of an American citizen, and while I felt that I was in duty bound to respect the laws of the land of my adoption, I could not, I cannot, and I never shall forget the land of my birth. I could not, while fighting in the armies of the United States, when face to face with those who would haul down and trample beneath their feet the flag of freedom, and baring my bosom to their bullets—I could not forget that I was born in another land—a land oppressed and tyrannized over. I cannot now forget it ; I never shall forget it. No matter what may be my fate here—I am still an Irishman, and while I have tried to be a faithful citizen of America, I am still an Irishman, with all the instincts of an Irishman. And let me remind your Honors, that it is my solemn conviction that if I were capable of forgetting the land of my birth, I would show myself to be unworthy the rights and privileges of an American citizen. I may have been imprudent in my endeavors to ameliorate the condition of my native land. There is a diversity of opinion on that subject, as there always must be upon such subjects. Had George Washington failed in his endeavors he would have been a rebel, and treated as a rebel by this tyrannical government that I would like to strike a blow against. I would like to remind your Honors that my native land has always been true to America. During the war of the Revolution, in America's sorest hour of trial, when most she needed a friend, when King George the Third sent to the Irish Parliament—for then, your Honors, Ireland had a Parliament of her own—and demanded men and money to put down the insurrection in America, that Irish Parliament, I am proud to say, voted that not a single man nor a single dollar should be given by Ireland to fight against Washington and his compatriots. Later still, after Ireland had been robbed of her Parliament, and during the late war, when Mason and Slidell were captured by an American seaman, England feeling that America was weak, and that the opportunity had come to strike her a deadly blow, threatened war against this country at a time when the North was poorly prepared to meet her, then it was that the people of Dublin, by the only means at their command, made known to England and to the world, that if she declared war against the land that had offered a home and an asylum to so many thousands of Irishmen, that the Irish people would be found battling upon the side of the struggling North. I contend, your Honors, that my native land has been always true to America. I contend that the men who stand before you to-day, charged with being violators of the law, every one of them was found in the ranks of the American army when it was necessary to defend the flag against those who would tear it down. On this account, while I cannot deny, and do not wish to deny that I have violated the law, I would ask you to be as lenient as possible, if not towards myself, at least towards those who have been brought into this trouble through my agency and instrumentality, and I here assume a reponsibility which does not properly belong to me. I was not the originator of the scheme of freeing Ireland by an invasion of Canada, though I have been one of its warmest supporters, and have advocated it from almost every platform from Maine to Minnesota. I am sorry to have to confess that the men who originated it, and who urged myself and others to take part in the endeavor, *basely* and *deliberalely* deserted us at the critical moment, and left us to our fate. For this I would like to see those men punished. I believe they deserve it, and if it were in my power, they should be punished. I shall caution my countrymen against them, and not only against them, but against any further efforts in this direction; and here I wish it to be distinctly understood, that my love for Ireland remains the same, and my hatred of that flag which to the Irish people is the symbol of tyranny and oppression, can never be changed. That flag I desire to tear down.

It has been said we had no right to go to Canada for the purpose of tearing it down, and that by attacking Canada we were injuring a people who had never injured us. Against those people we have no hostility; we have no hostility against the English people: it is the English government that we hate—it is the English government that we desire to fight. It is the flag that represents that government that we detest, and wherever it floats the Irish people, come weal or woe, claim the right to pull it down and trample it beneath their feet. It was prompted by this feeling that I attempted to invade Canada.

As the matter now stands, the invasion appears to have been a ridiculous farce. Had the attempt succeeded, it would have been otherwise.

I desire to say in conclusion, that whatever may have been my opinions heretofore—and I did believe that a successful attempt could have been made in that direction, I have believed it for years, and for years have labored to bring it about—I am now satisfied, however, that any further attempt would be highly criminal, because there is not the remotest chance of success. If there were, though I might go to the gallows to-morrow, I would tell my countrymen to go on; but I now believe that there is not, and I shall therefore advise them to desist; and so far as my influence will go, I will use it to convince the Irish people in America, that any farther attempt in that direction would be futile. Had I got out on bail before this trial, I should have travelled and used my influence to dissuade my friends from any further endeavors. Unfortunately, my friends did not understand my situation in time to bail me out, else I should have urged upon them to abandon the attempt, and to abandon it forever. Though I shall now be in prison, I shall use whatever influence I may have in that direction.

Apologizing to your Honors for detaining you so long, I will conclude by repeating, that I have always loved the laws of the land, that I have always been ready and willing to fight for them. I am ready and willing to fight for them now, as the honorable wound that I bear testifies I was in the past. This shall be my proudest recollection, and perhaps it may be the only legacy that I shall leave my children, the fact that their father fought and bled for this free land, which has offered a home and an asylum to so many thousands of the homeless and persecuted of Europe. It will always be my pride and pleasure' as long as life remains, that I have fought and bled for this the land of my adoption.

JUDGE WOODRUFF'S SENTENCE.

Judge Woodruff, in pronouncing sentence on Gen. O'Neill, said:

It would be a satisfaction to the Court if they had learned from the observations that you have seen fit to address us, that the regret which you have expressed (in so far as you allowed yourself to appear in any degree in the condition of a repentant criminal) had been founded upon a conviction that the offence which you have committed was a wrong; and if the regret expressed had not been placed upon a subsequent discovery of the fruitlessness of the effort in which you were engaged; and if it had exhibited in some higher degree a consciousness of the importance of the law which you have violated, and a respect which you have expressed in words, though disproved by a deliberate disregard of its injunctions.

The Court cannot suffer the importance of the law of the United States to be depreciated, which is designed, not immediately and directly for the benefit of another government or another people, but for the protection and maintenance of our own good faith, and the preservation of our own people from the evils which result to them from a disregard of its provisions; and which is essential to preserve them from entanglements and embarrassments in their intercourse with others, to which permission to violate this law with impunity would most certainly lead.

You have been charged with a violation of the law which forbids persons in our own territory from setting on foot a military expedition against a government or people of any other territory with which we are at peace. You have confessed your guilt. We have listened with a desire to give due heed to what you had to say respecting the judgment of the Court and the sentence which you should receive. To the suggestions that you have been misled by others, and that you were deceived, we can give no interpretation save this: that you were disappointed; that instead of finding a force adequate to secure a large measure of success to this expedition, and a support in men and supplies, and needed material aid, you found the force insignificant or the supplies deficient. and the support in all respects inadequate to the enterprise. In that you may have been deceived, but to state that you were thereby deceived is only to say that your purpose and expectation was to make that expedition effective to produce all the evil directly to the country invaded, by bringing upon it the desolation which war always brings, and incidentally to this country by involving it in the complications which were likely thence to ensue; so that the avowal of your disappointment is only the avowal of a purpose which magnifies the apparently trivial and insignificant endeavor which was made into an intention to engage in an enterprise in violation of the law, of singular and great importance.

The Court have listened to the history of your services in behalf of our own country, and in the maintenance of its laws, and the Court are not insensible to the claim which that service gave you, as it certainly did in the first instance, to the grateful regard of the government and people. But the Court cannot be insensible that the government and the people had a right to expect that one who had professed a desire to maintain the laws and sustain the government, should not lend his skill and his courage, either to plan, or to give life, energy or enthusiasm, to an enterprise in defiance of the laws; and, in some aspects of the case, the more you are exalted by the exhibition of courage, of military skill and successful achievements in the past, the greater is the crime when you prostitute that skill and courage and achievement by making it the instrument, or cause of inspiration, in the breast of others, and a stimulus to them under your leadership to engage in hostility towards a nation with which we are at peace. It thus becomes rather an aggravation.

It is suggested in your observations that you were stimulated by a sense of the oppression to which your countrymen have in years past been subjected. Any real or supposed wrong of your country or your countrymen furnishes no just vindication, though it may in a sort explain the insane folly and wickedness of making that the occasion of suffering and wrong to a people who are innocent of any share in the infliction of which you suppose that you and your people had cause to complain, and it is idle to say that not intending wrong to them you simply sought an injury to the government to which they owe allegiance. You have come into this court and avowed your guilt. The demands of justice require only that the infliction of punishment for your crime should be such as in our best judgment will serve to deter from a repetition of the offence, and as an example to prevent others from believing that they may repeat the offence with impunity. The Court may take notice of the history of the past, and aware of the leniency with which this offence was dealt some years ago, we are apprised that we are now dealing with its repetition in your person. The Court are not therefore at liberty to yield to considerations which might otherwise have influenced its judgment. I need hardly say that to those who are charged with the duty of administering justice, it is no pleasure, but, on the contrary, a pain, to advert to considerations which tend to anything like severity. They would be pleased, if personal gratification might be indulged, to accord even the extent of your request, by inflicting the lightest punishment the law would allow. They are nevertheless, by all considerations affecting their actions, and especially in dealing with a repetition of this offence in your person, constrained to make an example. The sentence of the Court, therefore, is that you be imprisoned in the State Prison of Vermont for the term of two years. But inasmuch as it is represented to the Court that you are not in a situation in which the infliction of a heavy fine would be productive of any other result than the probable extension of the period of detention, the Court are disposed to make the fine nominal. The statute requires that both be inflicted, and I add therefore the sentence that you pay a fine of ten dollars.

www.ingramcontent.com/pod-product-compliance
Lightning Source LLC
Chambersburg PA
CBHW021529090426
42739CB00007B/845

* 9 7 8 3 3 3 7 3 7 3 4 1 2 *